W
ALL THIN

[handwritten inscriptions, partly illegible]

Love - Best
wishes Adam
Kim
Joan - Norman
Atticoed
Dec. 1994

Nov. 1996

WITH GOD
ALL THINGS ARE POSSIBLE

Experiences of revival today

Melvin Banks

Marshall Pickering
An Imprint of HarperCollins*Publishers*

Marshall Pickering is an Imprint of
HarperCollins*Religious*
Part of HarperCollins*Publishers*
77–85 Fulham Palace Road, London W6 8JB

First published in Great Britain
in 1993 by Marshall Pickering

1 3 5 7 9 10 8 6 4 2

Copyright © 1993 Melvin Banks

Melvin Banks asserts the moral right to be
identified as the author of this work

A catalogue record for this book is
available from the British Library

ISBN 0 551 02801 7

Printed and bound in Great Britain by
HarperCollinsManufacturing Glasgow

Contents

To my precious Mother, Grace Banks, who prayed resurrection life back into my body on the riverbank, in May 1940, and who went to heaven in her 79th year on 23rd November 1992. I miss her every day.

"You were as good in my sight as an angel of God" – 1 Samuel 29:9

This ongoing work of the Holy Spirit is her greatest memorial.

INTRODUCTION

How great are his signs, how mighty his wonders! His kingdom is an eternal kingdom; his dominion endures from generation to generation.

(Daniel 4:3)

God is not a mere man as I am, that I should answer him; there is no umpire between us who might lay his hand upon us both.

(Job 9:32–33, Amplified Version)

In a revival, the first truth that comes to the fore is the fact that we see ourselves as God sees us.

The story goes of a minister visiting a household. The mother was preparing some tea for him when her four-year-old girl wandered up to the clergyman and commented, "You're not very handsome are you? In fact, you're very ugly!" He was quite stunned. When the mother came with tea and cakes, he told her what her offspring had said. The mother thought for a moment, then commented, "It's amazing how children come out with the truth, isn't it?"

God is showing us through his word all the facts we need to know both about himself, and about ourselves. God's divine truths are mirrors revealing, cleansing, illuminating, awakening, and *firing us up*. The Hebrew word for "revival" in Scripture literally means "to recover" or "to go back to".

Many Christians and churches for too long have been living at an abnormal spiritual level. Although converted, doctrinally correct, respectable, moral people, they have dwelt in a state of lethargy and sleepiness. By a new awareness of the Spirit of God, they are now seeing things as they *never saw them before*. From a background of backbiting, failure, weakness and constant criticism, *God is rousing and sweeping them to new peaks of challenge*. When God takes the stage, anything can happen, and he truly reveals to his people their genuine spiritual state.

In *The Wind of Fire*, my first book on the current revival in Britain, we saw that a phenomenon, a return to Pentecost and a fresh militant anointing is coming on a growing minority of God's people in a few scattered places. Believers energized by the Holy Spirit are beginning to shake the towns and villages of Britain.

In this present book I deal not so much with actual scenes of revival, or accounts of many conversions, blessing, deliverances, signs and wonders, but more with the salient truths, themes and lessons that God is re-revealing and imparting to us in this new wave and outpouring of the Spirit. It was Dr James Boswell, the famous seventeenth-century diarist, who remarked that "Men need to be reminded more than taught."

I am constantly asked by the curious, "What are the new emphases in teaching in this revival?" People are travelling long distances – even coming from other parts of the world – to see, learn, feel and hear what the Spirit is saying to us and to know what truths are being proclaimed.

GOD IS OPENING OUR EYES

A young lad was selling new-born puppies; his poster declared, "£5 a puppy". A gentleman came to view them; being newly born, they could not see. He noticed the low price, and said he would return the next day, as he would have to ask his wife what colour puppy she wanted. He returned the following day and was shocked to see that the price of the puppies was now £25 each! He declared, "This is scandalous! Why do they cost so much more today?" The lad perkily replied, "Well, yesterday they couldn't see, but now they can. They're worth much more with their eyes open!"

In revival God opens our eyes again to many hitherto forgotten or neglected truths. That is what this book is really about. *It is God's truth that sets the people free*. The blessings of the Lord are obtained only by strict regard to his word, obedience to his truths and knowledge and practice of his statutes and teachings.

The following remarkable prophecy about the present revival was spoken out at a recent prayer seminar:

God is speaking forth his will, God is speaking forth his plan, God is speaking forth his purpose.

You are giving birth to that great move of his Spirit. The way you give birth is through soul-travail and intercessory prayer.

The Spirit of God is enlisting men and women who will switch off the TV, ignore the phone, forgo the overtime, cast off the trivial, cease the time-wasting activities, and volunteer for this task, to come aside and lie before him at his feet.

He is seeking out today those who will respond. The work has begun, the revival is here in its infancy, but it is now up to you. . .

The darkness that hovers on the horizon of our nation will be dispelled and driven back. The blessing of God has come, the rivers are flowing. He is bringing life, salvation, regeneration, health, joy, peace, reconciliation and healing. The floodgates are slowly opening, being released on the land again. It is so, it will be so.

Isaiah, at the start of the revival in his day, "saw the Lord high and lifted up". Moses, records the writer of the epistle to the Hebrews, "endured by seeing him who is invisible". The revival has started with a fresh vision of the magnified, glorified, mighty, precious, loving, glorious Lord of Lords and King of Kings. This wonderful God is revealing more and more to us about his timeless truth.

After years of preparation, suddenly, just a few years ago, we began to see God's miracle-working power being manifested on an unparalleled scale. God sent fire on groups of people who were seeking his vindication and glory. They blew the trumpet in Zion, for the name of the Lord has been insulted. God's honour had been abused, but they sought God's greater glory.

Only he can send the fire of revival, and only he can maintain the fire of revival. It is his work, but he uses human vessels.

THE HEART OF THE REVIVAL

The heart of revival is making Jesus Lord. To have a revival you don't need a clique of super-saints — you need born-again, Christ-centred, Holy-Ghost-filled, soul-winning disciples.

The revival churches are not ordinary churches, but *extraordinary churches!* God has not abandoned his seeking people. God is calling us *to be more, not only to do more.* We are God's messengers to a storm-tossed world. God is shaking us out of our complacency and restoring us to a true fear of the Lord. So much of evangelical faith has for generations been mere words with little power and no revival fire. Our churches have been holy islands of folk, happy with their respectable little congregations of 150–200, surrounded by a vast sea of hell-bound sinners.

For revival our ultimate foundation is Jesus. He must take complete precedence in our lives: we must be totally in love with him. He must be in charge of your emotions and your money and your time. As you give yourself humbly to the Lord and to your fellows, the Spirit will work in and through you. If I hadn't seen the Spirit doing this in thousands of lives over the past years, then I couldn't preach about it. Those unwilling to surrender, to be crucified to self, to be obedient to God and to change their ways, are being bypassed in this present wave of God's Spirit.

Evangelical Christians get an enormous amount of good teaching. In the UK there are more people *per capita* teaching the word of God than in any other country in the world, including the USA. British Christians have been spoiled and pampered in this respect, and I fear that has caused many to become indolent and settled down. Harold Horton used to say, "God never blesses lazy bones." God is calling us to courage, daring, faith, to cross Jordan and bring down the walls of Jericho. If we don't risk all and enter the promised land, we will never know its quality of life, which is *victorious living.* C. T. Studd said, "God is not looking for nibblers of the possible, but for grabbers of the impossible." We must be as willing as Caleb was to dare, to gamble and to trust. You just cannot read the Old or the New Testament without coming across men who were gamblers for God.

Don't get the idea that I am a courageous daredevil for God, ready to go anywhere. Far from it! Down inside me is a deep, deep fear of the unknown. But I do believe that the Spirit of God produces courage in the life of the believer. I do know for sure that I wouldn't have got anywhere at all in the Christian life if I hadn't been prepared to gamble, to say to the Lord, "Well, I haven't got much faith, and I'm not very strong, and I don't know much, but . . . I'll go. I believe that somehow you'll hold it together."

"BE STRONG AND VERY COURAGEOUS"

Avoid phrases like, "If only. . ." Such an attitude drains away your strength. Some Christians have exchanged their backbones for wishbones. Paul wrote, "Therefore, my dear brothers, stand firm. Let nothing move you" (1 Corinthians 15:58). If you look at people you'll be disappointed. If you worry about situations you'll get discouraged. If you think of yourself you'll get depressed. Look to Jesus, however, and you'll be able *to get up and go on from victory to victory. Keep on keeping on.* Don't let yourself be thrown by past defeats. Don't keep on fretting about things which have humiliated or depressed you. Don't keep on feeling guilty once the time of repentance is past. Regret can be one of the most subtle forms of self-love. It is not the road to humility, but the road to self-absorption. We are indeed unworthy servants, but we are also Spirit-filled kings, priests of God. As we fix our attention upon our glorious Lord, and offer him our worship, we will know the encouragement which he offers. It is God's will to work in our lives and to bless us in one way or another.

Face disappointment, disillusionment, delay and the declining years and realize that they are part of God's means to encourage you to reach out for greater faith, compassion and ability. Face danger with joyful daring. Use your doubts. Cultivate dependability, that you may disciple other people more effectively.

God said to Joshua: "Be strong and very courageous. Be careful to obey all the law my servant Moses gave you; do not turn from it to the right or to the left, that you may be successful wherever you go. Do not let this Book of the Law depart from your mouth; meditate on it day and night, so that you may be careful to do everything written in it. Then you will be prosperous and successful. Have I not commanded you? Be strong and courageous. Do not be terrified; do not be discouraged, for the Lord your God will be with you wherever you go" (Joshua 1:7–9).

Remember – today's mighty oak is yesterday's little nut that held its ground. The devil's strategy for stopping the forward movement of the Gospel is to seek to deceive us, to undermine our confidence in the divine word, for Satan knows only too well that we get the presence of God in and through obedience to God's words. *We must act on God's commands, cleave to Christ, cling to the Holy Spirit.*

Melvin Banks
The Homestead,
Monks Way,
Chippenham, Wilts.
June 1993

— 1 —

THE FIRE BURNS ON

It was a bored smile that met me, as I tried to explain the revival in simple terms to the ITV crew visiting one of my revival meetings in the south of England. Strenuous though my efforts were, my explanation of what God was doing just seemed to fall on deaf ears. I remembered the words of a preacher of a previous generation: "If you can explain a revival, then it is *not* a revival!"

They asked the usual bland questions:

"How much money is being made?"

"None," I replied.

"Isn't it extreme Americanism?"

"No, it's not from the USA – it's from heaven!"

"Isn't there a lot of hysterical emotionalism at your meetings?"

"No, the things which are happening are just a repetition of what happened in the Bible!"

The crowds thronged the long afternoon service. Almost the total audience became converted for the first time. There was weeping and laughter; peace swept over people, and some jumped for joy; then came a wave of God's Spirit in healing.

As I laid hands on one woman, she suddenly cried out, "I can see! I can see!" The woman, who had been blind for some years, pointed towards the ITV camera. "That's a camera!" she declared. The puzzled, startled TV men moved closer. She pointed to the TV interviewer. "You have a moustache!" she cried out. "Look at those flowers!" The huge crowd clapped, cheered and cried. Later she told the TV people, "I've never been to a meeting like this before. I'd heard that extraordinary things were happening, so I came to give it a try." She wasn't a well-versed charasmatic full of Bible texts, but an average "sinner", looking for help, hoping for a miracle.

Holy Ghost power had flooded the building. It was out of this world! The TV interviewer and his team ran from row to row, from person to person, trying to record the amazing things that were happening. A man discards his neck brace and waves it in the air. He no longer needs it, as the disease and pain in his neck have been removed by God's power.

The next day these events are broadcast just after the 6.00 p.m. National News. Well over one million people see them in the major cities of southern England. These very revival scenes – hundreds of conversions, instant miracles, empty wheelchairs, interviews of people who have received joy, release, forgiveness and healing from God – are being carried into countless thousands of homes coast to coast. *Revival is touching the nation's heart.*

There is no doubt, in spite of the fierce controversy, that the ripples of revival are spreading ever more widely across the land. Some are for it, others are against it; some cannot recognize it, but others are losing themselves in the Spirit's floodwaters. *The fire is burning on.* This is only the tip of the iceberg – just a sample of what God has in store for us in his magnificent plans for the future. The revival will spread from street to street, from town to town, from village to village. The country lanes and the huge tenements of the inner cities will echo to the sound of the singing, praising, worshipping and shouting of those whose hearts have been changed by God's grace.

"THIS IS A DAY OF GOOD NEWS"

The fire burns on in a few, but most Christians in the UK still need to be touched by *God's heat.* I am reminded of the four men who left God's people behind in the doomed city of Samaria when the wicked Ben-Hadad was besieging it (see 2 Kings 7). The inhabitants of Samaria were so short of food that a donkey's head fetched eighty shekels of silver, while a bowlful of seed pods sold for five shekels (2

Kings 6:25). The people even started to eat their own children (6:28–29)!

Yet by supernatural sounds (7:6–7) God brought fear upon the enemy and chased the vast genocidal army out of his land overnight. But God's people still thought they were at the mercy of the enemy. How like the modern church! So many of the believers in this country think the devil still holds sway. They think there is no hope. Christians are starving due to poor teaching or a lack of deep commitment to the Scriptures.

But as the people of Samaria sat in the city starving, there was food and plenty only a few hundred metres away! *The enemy was scattered*, death was conquered, God had sent a revival, the hunger was over (7:8). The four men went into the tents of the enemy and found there food and plenty, gold and silver in armfuls. They had all the riches of the Gentiles. We too have power, revival, spiritual life, God's word, energy, joy, riches and health – *all good things are ours!* "He will fill the empty with good things". We have all the favourable promises of God, yet most of his church in Britain still lives outside his word, outside his revival. They have missed, or deny, or do not avail themselves of the fire that burns on.

Are you starving, fruitless, missing your gifts, your inheritance? We must blow the trumpet in Zion, shake the gates of brass, chase the enemy out of the camp. We must not wait and starve! As the old saying goes, God's people sit in church singing, "I'm standing on the promises", when they are in fact sitting on the premises! A whole city and nation is starving, while there is wine, meat, food and abundance only a prayer away. Bob Geldoff challenged the world during the Ethiopian famine of the eighties. He said, "People are dying – what are *you* doing about it?"

The four men said to each other, "*We are not doing right. This is a day of good news and we are keeping it to ourselves.*" Millions are starving, revival has begun, but God's people in the UK are keeping the Good News to themselves! Multitudes live in a nightmare of darkness, yet God's children are withholding the Good News of Christ. John Wesley said, "The church has nothing to do but save souls." J. B. Philips wrote, "The Gospel is nothing but a frozen asset unless it is communicated."

Methods, ideas, systems and gimmicks have failed in Britain. We must return to the Bible, to the message of the Cross. We must speed the Good News of joy and supernatural power to all men, with renewed enthusiasm. God is giving us decisive victory; vindicating power is ours; nothing can halt the progress of dedicated, holy characters, burning for God. He is giving us extraordinary ascendancy. We are not the church cooped up in some theological retreat house; we are not a candle in a dungeon but a city set upon a hill! *The Bridegroom is returning*, the rider on his white horse is on the horizon. We must live worthily.

THE DEVIL IS DEFEATED

In the revival our problem is to accommodate the vast crowds that come. The resurrection of Jesus has come down, the cosmic King of Kings is amongst us, to turn *his* church from shallow defeatism into the almighty power of God. Descending unheralded, it has come suddenly to us who are so undeserving. The deadly mists of doubt are lifting, and a beautiful new spring morning is beginning. "Them that have sat in darkness have seen a great light." Thousands are being set free, and are rediscovering the old truths of God. *There is a return to Pentecost*. The devil is defeated. As Reinhardt Bonnke has put it, "The devil is a mouse with a microphone." Jesus said, "I have given you authority to trample on snakes and scorpions, and to overcome all the power of the enemy; nothing will harm you" (Luke 10:19).

A burglar in London was getting over a wall after robbing a house, dragging a large sack of "goodies" which he had lifted, when he came almost face to face with a policeman. He made off in the opposite direction, the bobby in hot pursuit. The officer, however, was rather overweight and near to retirement, so he was very slow! The young thief was getting away. But in his spare time the copper entertained kiddies at their parties with impersonations. He was very good at animal sounds, particularly dogs. So in the darkness he threw his voice, barking loudly like a Rottweiler. The criminal heard this vicious snarl on his heels, and ran faster. But it got louder and fiercer, so fearfully he cast down his stolen goods and raised his hands in surrender. The exhausted constable finally caught him up, and handcuffed the culprit. The burglar looked round everywhere for the nasty hound, but could see no dog! He had a bark but no bite!

The devil has no bite for the Christian believer living in his inheritance. The devil is defeated, he's beneath our feet. No darkness, guilt, temptation, fear, curse, habit, obsession or sin can master us. As Christian entered the castle in Bunyan's immortal story, the fierce lions at the gate put trepidation into him, but as he looked closer, he noticed that they had no teeth, no claws, no fangs. They had all been pulled out at Calvary! Jesus Christ has "disarmed the powers and authorities" (Colossians 2:15). The devil has no bite. We have "all power in heaven and in earth" through Jesus Christ. "We are more than conquerors." "No weapon forged against us will prosper." The church must rise up and defeat its innumerable enemies!

SLEEPING CHRISTIANS

Have our ministers sold out the Gospel for professional advantage? The anointing has been diluted, as far too many have cooled down for their own denominational advancement and promotion!

In his story *The Silver Chair* C. S. Lewis tells of God's children being beguiled by the wicked witch of the underworld. The "thrum, thrum, thrum" of her guitar has wooed them to sleep. What a picture of the church today! Only a few have kept the vision of Aslan the Lion (Christ) and not forgotten his true message. A million believers have been wooed to sleep by the "thrum, thrum, thrum" of the guitar. God's people have drifted into cosy Christianity, into a crossless, costless faith.

Thousands of leaders and believers have been drugged by apathy, worldliness, love of possessions, idolatry, soft religion. Even evangelicals have fallen asleep. Fearful and cautious about biblical commitment and miraculous New Testament faith, they have come to a halt. Renewal is okay, *but not revival*. They want revival only on their terms, in their way. But "The wind blows wherever it pleases" (John 3:8). In Lewis' story only the Marsh-wiggle dares to "put his foot in the fire"; as a result he comes alive and remembers the words of Aslan, shakes the children awake and leads them out. Is your foot in the fire? Have you caught fire? Or have you been a rebel? Have you compromised?

Repentance is a key word in Scripture. The Laodi-
cean church was guilty not of drunkenness or
immorality, but of a lukewarm heart and of smug
satisfaction with their material wealth. Many of us
need to repent in these two areas. Look at what the
Lord told them: "Those whom I love I rebuke and
discipline. So be earnest, and repent" (Revelation
3:19).

Many try to ignore or oppose this revival. I have
news for you, reader. In my studies I've found that
in every revival since the time of the Apostles people
have questioned it, denied it, argued against it.
There was opposition to the revivals of the modern
era: the Wesleyan Revival, the Salvation Army
Revival of the late 1870s, the Ulster Revival, the
Welsh Revival of 1904, the Hebrides Revival of
1950.

Are you feeling discouraged? Do you desperately
need to have your spiritual passion restored? For
many of us, life is cluttered up with things. *We have
settled down.* However loudly the Lord may call,
we cannot travel immediately and gladly in a fresh
direction. No wonder one cynic has described the
church as the "best disguised set of pilgrims the
world has ever seen". But this is true not only of
material prosperity. Spiritual blessing can also be a
hindrance. A glorious experience of the Lord can
become yesterday's idol that we keep revisiting,

instead of a day-to-day spur to holy living. To be a pilgrim is to go through the valley of Baca, be it arid or lush. It is to have your eyes on the far horizon. It is to go on despite the discouragements and the delights of life. It is to persevere. The psalmist describes pilgrims as those "whose strength is in you", who "go from strength to strength" (Psalm 84:5, 7).

Life need not be a boring routine with each new day much the same as the last. For the revived believer, the imagination of his mind and the yearning of his heart are fixed on the one great objective. *His heart and his flesh cry out for the living God, the Lord almighty, his sun and shield, his King and his God.* The Bible has many ways of describing the Christian life. The believer is spoken of as a runner committed to a race (Hebrews 12:1–2), a steward entrusted with gifts (Matthew 25:14), a soldier engaged in war (2 Timothy 2:3), a servant called to a life of obedience (John 15:20).

GETTING BACK TO BASICS

The revival is getting back to basics. In this book we re-learn what God is bringing back to tens of thousands in the UK today. Havner said, "Revival is the saints getting back to normal." The present revival is original, biblical, apostolic Christianity. Our people are convinced that their authority is the

Bible. We affirm the supreme authority of Scripture over the traditions of the church and over the opinions of the individual. That is our first hallmark. The great strength of the whole movement is that we are committed to the truth. We believe that the Gospel is the truth of God.

We refuse to compromise concerning the uniqueness of Jesus Christ. The more pluralistic society becomes, with different ethnic groups and different religions, the more urgent it is for Christians to affirm the absolute supremacy, uniqueness and finality of our Lord and Saviour, Jesus Christ. He has no peers, no rivals, no successors. He is Jesus the Only One. There is nobody like him and we must never surrender that truth.

It is like a country garden competition. A husband and wife team got their garden just perfect. They did not know when the local judge was coming to look at the garden. Each morning the wife would say to the husband, "What about the weeds? Have you cut the grass? Have you collected the stray leaves? Have you trimmed the edges? Are the plants tied up? What about the borders? I wonder if the judge will come today." Every day we wait for the Lord of Glory, the great Judge of the earth, to come. Do not miss the last great revival – it has begun. Are your weeds taken up? Is your life clean? Are you scrupulously honest? Is your life straight? Are you ready? Are you keeping the fire burning?

The revival is Jesus coming again to this generation. Every revival is his return with power and glory. As Wallis puts it, in revivals "All human personalities are over-shadowed, man is in the background and God is taking the field." His presence is enough to dispel our fear, defeat doubt and deal with anxiety.

We have distanced ourselves from God. Even Christians have been half-hearted in this past generation; even "renewed" believers have gone only so far. A white-hot, loving passion for souls has been a rarity.

Shakespeare made one of his characters say, "He hath a daily beauty that makes me ugly." Compared to God we are ugly. We are wanting, we are impure, we are unjust. He is the mirror that shows up all our spots, wrinkles, warts and darknesses. As Jeremiah put it: "The heart is deceitful above all things and beyond cure" (Jeremiah 17:9). The sinless beauty and awesome presence of Christ is disturbing. It's rather like Hans Christian Andersen's story of the Emperor who thought he was dressed in a fine uniform, but was in fact walking around naked! In God's sight we have nothing to commend us. We are barren, blighted, self-righteous, dry, carnal, unclean failures! As Disraeli said, "Man is a good thing spoiled."

But in Christ there is glorious hope for us! In this revival those who were worthless, unfruitful, wandering, discouraged, disappointed, critical and ungracious rebels have become sons, victors, earth-movers and overcomers! God is looking for such a people. A tiny, growing minority who live by faith are moving society and shaking this land. God will do anything for such daring, loving, believing dedicated people. God is looking for folk who believe what he says. In the new, mighty, ongoing, spreading Pentecostal revival God is bringing us into his fire, out of past failures, hurts, breakdowns and disappointments. God is raising up new regiments of his people, who are willing to lay down their lives for Christ, to kneel before the pure splendour of the Cross, and to submit to the burning, cleansing, refining, purging flame of God's spirit.

A PASSION FOR HOLINESS

We are learning that there must be a new, rich closeness to God in our lives, if we are to know his fire and to stay in his fire. All the things that spoil us come to the fore. There is a new passion for holiness. Evil habits, false beliefs, occult practices, doubt, bitterness, misery, fear – these things become like a gravestone round our necks. We long to be completely free of all carnality. We're welcomed back in to God's close family, we have a new sense of direct divine participation in our lives. God's love becomes real to us; the marvellous person of Jesus is a living daily reality and wonder to us.

We live in the reality of the Spirit's power, we bask in the company of Jesus. He is the best company to keep: he is the truth of God, the very life of God. God's kingly rule begins in your life in revival. There is a fervent expectation; there is no morbid, formal, dull religious living. Jesus gets closer and closer to you. He is always available, approachable, loving, generous, wanting to hug you, wanting to enfold you in his arms and welcome you home!

We lose blandness and ignorance, we see Jesus' beauty. The character of Jesus becomes immensely attractive to us. The supernatural miracles and wonders which we see at the revival meetings are exciting, but most wonderful of all is the experience of Jesus' mighty, consuming presence – often startling, always awesome. *Christ is all!* Powerful preaching sweeps the decks clean. Richard Baxter said, "If we can but teach Christ to our people, we teach them all." We are getting back to health, as we ailing believers wake up and focus on Christ!

The four men in 2 Kings 7 said to each other, "We're not doing right. This is a day of good news and we are keeping it to ourselves." This could be said of many parts of the church in the British Isles in the latter decades of this century. We have especially failed to reach the ethnic minorities who live in our midst. The Buddhists, Hindus, Moslems,

Sikhs and Rastafarians have been almost totally unreached, unloved, unbridged, unevangelized. We have kept the Good News to ourselves!

However, the current revival is reaching thousands of Hindus, Moslems and Sikhs with the glorious Gospel. This nation has not seen for sixty or seventy years such a manifestation of God's Spirit among unchurched people. In Coventry recently a thousand Hindus, Moslems and Sikhs queued up for hours to get into a Gospel meeting. The local Assemblies of God church members, longing for more of the Lord's power, had been praying day and night and had reached out into the city. As a result Asian people flocked to the meeting with their families and sat and listened for hours to the Gospel of the blood and power of our Lord Jesus Christ! That evening the enquiry rooms were packed with people seeking salvation from the Lord. Two thousand received healing. The Hindu community was electrified!

The revival has come in power to a certain West Midlands church which happens to be next door to a public house. The pub is very popular, drawing hundreds of customers from a wide area. Before the revival came its patrons treated the nearby church with indifference. But when the revival came, people formed in queues to get in to the church, and the singing drowned out the pub's amusement machines and honky-tonk piano! Soon miracles happened and became known throughout the city. At about 9.15 p.m. each night, the patrons poured out on to the kerbs outside the pub to watch the people streaming out of the church for the next hour or so. Many were pushing their wheelchairs or carrying their crutches and hospital sticks. The people from the pub cheered at these sights, and some later came to the revival meetings.

Ask yourself: Am I seeing revival like this in my church? Where is my church failing? Why are we not moving in God's power like this? Are we adequately reaching the unchurched people of our nation?

TOO MUCH TALK!

Luke, the author of the Acts of the Apostles, in his account of Paul's visit to Athens, makes this somewhat caustic comment about the people of that city: "All the Athenians and the foreigners who lived there spent their time doing nothing but talking about and listening to the latest ideas" (Acts 17:21). Is that a good description of much of church life today? What is the latest fad in the church? What is the new phase that is upon us? What is your church "in to"? Praise and worship? Wimberism? Shepherding? Fatherhood teaching? Faith and prosperity? The restoration of the church? Dancing "before the Lord"? Drama? Body ministry? Overhead projection? Casting out demons? Inner healing? Sibrinski teaching? "Breathing" or "blowing" on people? Instant prophets? Falling "in the Spirit"? "Name and claim it"? Some of these are helpful things, some are not beneficial, and others are downright ludicrous!

So much talk, talk, talk... Only in a few places is a passion for souls paramount. God has shrunk in the estimation of most ministers and churches in the UK today. They are in a rut! In the outback of Australia a poster in the desert reads: "Choose your rut carefully – you'll be in it for the next 2,000 miles!" Many churches are in a rat-race, a round of spiritual events, a rut, going round in circles. God is wanting to stir up our expectancy, confidence and outreach. He wants his love, freedom and Spirit to be shared by all men. Many people in our land are living in a nightmare, without hope. But God's people are beginning to occupy territory once held by the powers of darkness. Thousands are being changed by Jesus. He does not take the technicolour out of life – he puts it in! He is wiping away tears and setting many free!

Listen, obey, bathe in his love, go with his Word ... that is the key. Share *him* with everyone. From Genesis to Revelation, the great Love Epic of the ages moves from eternity to eternity. God cries, "I have loved you with an everlasting love" (Jeremiah 31:3); "How can I give you up? ... My heart is

changed within me; all my compassion is aroused"
(Hosea 11:8). He is seeking lost men. His people
must be a people of *godly love* for all mankind, for
the folk in the next street, for the neighbours down
the road, for the people you do business with and
work alongside.

God is a consuming fire. He is all love, a furnace
of love burning for his creatures. Whenever we carry
the Gospel, it must be because we care. We are not
to heal for the sake of seeing a wonder. God is not
in showbusiness. Jesus didn't come to earth to make
a name for himself. The Lord told them he loved
them because of his love for them — which is no
reason at all! The reason for love is love, which is
God himself. Love is not God, but God is love.

Jesus amazes me. He healed the man at the pool
of Bethesda and went away and never even said
who he was. What advantage did that healing bring
him? No glory, no fame; in fact, it brought him
trouble and persecution (John 5). He took a deaf
man, and led him by the hand ouside the village so
nobody would see, restoring his hearing. He did the
same with a blind man. He restored others and
told them not to say a word. There is only one
explanation for his entire work, and that is that he
loved people. It's profound compassion which he
wants us to share.

GOOD NEWS SHOULD BE SHARED

I shall never forget hearing that intrepid missionary to China, the late Mildred Cable, addressing a crowded meeting in Liverpool's Central Hall. She and her missionary companions were the first women to cross the fearsome Gobi Desert in Mongolia. I shall always remember her challenging words: "The unforgivable sin of the desert is to know where water is, and never tell anyone about it."

Good news should always be shared. In Isaiah 40, the prophet tells the Jewish people, who have been living in exile in Babylon, that at long last they are to return to their homeland. Good news indeed, and something of the thrill of the prophet's words is conveyed to us in that glorious tenor solo in Handel's *Messiah*, "Comfort ye, comfort ye, my people, saith your God." Good news is always welcome.

The New Testament begins with Good News. It tells of those "glad tidings of great joy" which heralded the coming of Christ. When the shepherds, who first heard those tidings, had been to Bethlehem, they could not keep such wonderful news to themselves. Luke tells us that "all who heard it were amazed at what the shepherds said to them" (Luke 2:18).

We recall that it was Mary Magdalene who ran

in the early dawn light from Joseph's garden with the news that Jesus had risen from the dead.

Our Lord's commission to his disciples just before the Ascension was that they should go and share the Good News with every nation. They went! They could not and did not keep silent.

We recall the account in Acts 5 of how the apostles were arrested and brought before the Council for preaching in the name of Jesus, when they had been strictly forbidden to do so. Peter and the others told their accusers that they must obey God rather than men. We are told how they were threatened again and flogged. Verses 41–42 tell us the sequel: "The apostles left the Sanhedrin, rejoicing because they had been counted worthy of suffering disgrace for the Name. Day after day, in the temple court and from house to house, they never stopped teaching and proclaiming the good news that Jesus is the Christ."

We must never forget that it was through the faithful, continuing witness of the early Christian church that the Good News reached our own shores. So we must carry it out to all men and women.

The question is, have you shared the Good News? When did you last seek to share the Good News of God's love as revealed in Jesus with someone who really needed to hear it? When the Samaritan woman met Jesus, she ran all the way back to her home village to share her wonderful experience. She was so thrilled by this encounter that she left her water-pot at the well. That could wait until later! Do I share her eagerness to tell anyone about my Lord? This kind of sharing is far removed from the off-putting practice of "trying to push religion down people's throats". Witnessing to our faith should be a natural, happy thing.

When Lord Coggan, formerly Archbishop of Canterbury, was Bishop of Bradford, he went to visit Canada. During one of his addresses he used an illustration which all Canadians would understand and appreciate. He said: "The trouble with some Christians is that they are like the St Lawrence River in wintertime – frozen at the mouth!"

There are many ways of sharing the Good News. Sometimes it will be by word of mouth, sometimes by giving or lending someone an interesting Christian book – love will always find a way! We can share the Gospel by kindness, by babysitting for neighbours, by inviting them out for a meal or maybe to a Full Gospel Businessmen's chapter dinner, or by getting them to a "Miracle" service. One million people a year accept invitations to attend my crusades. Out of twelve million invitations to the people of the UK in the last ten years to attend one of our evangelistic services, only two have been sent back to us – both by humanists! In areas where they have torn up Gospel tracts, thrown them back or refused them, every household will take a Gospel leaflet with miracles on it! In large IRA strongholds in Ireland, where Protestant preachers could be shot, thousands of my leaflets were given out, and only one family refused one – and even they later came to a Gospel meeting! The leaflets were received with great interest, and hundreds of people came from these huge republican estates to sit and hear about Christ and salvation in the revival services. *People want to know*.

JESUS IS AMONGST US NOW!

The One who burst out of the grave, emptied the tomb, scattered his enemies, leapt into Hades, set captives free, spoiled principalities and powers, gave gifts unto men, made a conquering comeback, turned the tide in the universe, routing the devil and evil forever, *is amongst us now!*

How thrilling it is when during one of our revival campaigns a town, village or suburb experiences a notable outpouring of the Holy Spirit! The area is saturated and shaken by the Gospel; the gates of hell are unhinged in that district, and the devil and his works are routed! Sometimes as much as a fifth of the town comes to the meetings – even in pagan, non-church, working-class, spiritually apathetic communities.

As the campaign workers and I drive out of the

town, people wave to us from the roadsides. Everyone shakes our hands – they all know someone who has been saved or healed in the revival. They all say, "Come back again soon!" It seems impossible that anyone in the whole district could not have heard of the signs and wonders and the power of our Lord Jesus Christ!

A Holy Ghost storm has broken upon us! The chorus we sing at the revival meetings goes:

The church of God is moving,
The battle has been won,
The foe is overcome.
We are marching on today,
We'll say "Goodbye" to doubt
And give a victory shout!
The church of God is moving. . .

Is your heart burning for the lost? God bids us all to go with the message! Will you join his great army? Will you make him the Captain of your salvation? If we are to be strong, happy, useful, loving, committed, winning Christians, we must readily say: "I will stand for him, I will unfurl the banner of the Cross. I am ready. He can count on me!"

2

ALL SORTS OF PEOPLE

I had just led a Sunday afternoon revival meeting at a little church in a small West Country town. About fifty people had attended; two thirds were visitors, and mostly non-church people. I prayed, then preached, and saw a number come for help, counsel and prayers. As I got into my car after the meeting, one of the helpers ran out to waylay me, even though it was streaming down with rain. He hugged me through the car window and thanked me for coming.

I smiled and said, "It's been a pleasure to be with you. Don't forget to thank the Lord every day. Follow it up, and keep praying, praising and spreading the Good News."

"Do you know who we saw converted this afternoon?" he said, with bright, wide eyes. I wondered who it could be. The local Bobby? Or the "black sheep" of the village, who had at last repented? It was "one of the Great Train Robbers!" I was told. What news!

He was one of the gang who had robbed the Royal Mail train in 1963. He had spent many years in prison. He was a tough, hard man, but now he had given his life to God. He had found redemption through the Living Christ. He had also been healed of asthma, which was what he had originally come to be prayed for. Nothing is too hard for God!

In the present revival the power of almighty God is touching all sorts of people, from different backgrounds and with different needs. Jesus showed no partiality. Whatever your past has been, through Jesus you can find a way back to the Father, and you can live to glorify God. He is all-powerful to break every stronghold of past sin. God can free every sinner who desires to be set free. God delights to forgive us.

The revival is proving to be life-changing for some famous people and for countless unknown folk. As the Word says, "the kingdom of heaven is like a net that was let down into the lake and caught all kinds of fish" (Matthew 13:47).

A MAYOR IS CONVERTED

I was in a famous city on the east coast. Nine hundred people packed the building to total capacity. We all stood as the Mayor entered the hall. She had never been to a meeting like this before. She sat on the platform and the meeting continued unabated, as if there was no earthly dignitary there. People worshipped the Lord, raising hands, jumping with joy, crying openly, falling on their knees, praying aloud, dancing in the aisles.

Eventually the time came for me to speak. I preached on the power of the blood of Jesus, telling the old-fashioned, Holy Ghost message which has been proclaimed since the time of the early church. Holy Spirit breezes fell upon us, people shouted, others affirmed their faith with exuberant "Amens". God's power was cutting like a knife as I made an appeal for those without faith, without peace, without hope of heaven, to throw their all on God. Scores of people responded, and I was thrilled to see that the Mayor was among them! As we repeated the prayer of repentance and commitment and surrender to the living Jesus, the Mayor said the prayer along with all the others.

She watched eagerly as a young girl, who had been crippled by arthritis, now ran up the aisle, dancing and jumping. I had laid hands on her and our Lord Jesus Christ had wonderfully healed her. The Mayor, with tears in her eyes, saw many, many people healed that night. She will never forget the hour her heart was warmed and changed.

THE WORST MAN IN TOWN

I was preaching in a small Cornish town eighteen months ago. Before the service an elderly lady approached me. She began to talk slowly in a deep Cornish accent: "Yer the gent, aren't yer, who does the healing bit, to help us?"

"Well," I replied, "I pray for sick people, and the good Lord above does heal many folk."

"That be it. Well, yer se, it's 'im down there" – she pointed to a man who stood some metres away listening. "That be my husband. He's sick, with a very bad spine, and the hospital at Truro can't do anything for him, so I thought I would get him to see yer."

I replied, "Well, I'm happy that you have come, and we shall pray hard for him."

Leaning over, she said in a whisper, "Well, it be like this, you see, Reverend – he's never been to church for nearly fifty years, not since we got married. I got him in for the wedding, but he's never been back since, not until tonight. It's a bloomin' miracle that he's come!" With that she shuffled off.

Soon the hall was crowded. At that service many people were saved and healed. Then the little old man made his way slowly forward, "If yer can do anything with this back of mine, Reverend, I'd be that grateful," he said. Within minutes God's Spirit came on that rough old Cornishman who had not

given God more than a few passing thoughts for
half a century. Then suddenly he shouted, "By golly,
it's been and gone, look yer!" He showed us his
instant freedom by bending, shaking a leg and doing
a dance. Everybody was laughing; his wife was
weeping with joy. There was no doubt that God
loved this tough old man! He went home without
a pain, and has not had one since.

The dear old fellow found Christ that night and
has never missed fellowship in God's house since.
He never had to be followed up, he followed us up!
After the service, as people were going off home,
someone came up to me, introducing himself as a
local man who had lived in the town all his life. He
had witnessed the miracle to "Old Ben". He said,
"You don't realize just what a miracle that was
tonight, Melvin – that man is regarded as the worst
man in town! He's often under the influence of
alcohol. His sons are in and out of prison, often
fighting in the pubs. It's a treble miracle!"

Time and again Jesus embraced the ones whom
society had rejected; he restored their dignity.
David, after he had committed adultery and murder,
was forgiven by God. Jonah was brought back from
his wanderings and given great success. Jesus turned
the tax fiddler Zacchaeus into an honest, upright,
generous, benevolent man. The vicious, bad-tem-
pered Peter was turned into a pioneer of new
churches. The murderer Saul of Tarsus was appre-

hended on the Damascus Road by God's light, and was redeemed and reconciled to become the greatest lover of souls who ever lived, next to Jesus. The dying thief, a rogue rejected even by the high-handed, violent Romans as the worst of criminals, was made a saint fit for Paradise and was personally welcomed into the Kingdom by Jesus Christ himself! In the present revival we are seeing the same thing happening: God is accepting and saving those whom society rejects.

Jesus is not just a great man or a superior angel, he is someone far more wonderful – he is the Son of God, the Lord of Glory. Weak, lost, helpless sinners need a powerful Saviour, and this is the kind of person Jesus Christ is. He is not like others, who may try to help us but are powerless to do so. He cannot fail. We can trust him. It is God who has come to the rescue.

People in our own generation are surrounded by what Bertrand Russell called an "unyielding despair". I have heard many people curse the day of their birth, saying, "I wish I had never been born!" But I have never heard anyone curse the day of their new birth! Many cry out with the Psalmist, "My guilt has overwhelmed me like a burden too heavy to bear" (Psalm 38:4). But Jesus offers relief, freedom from the murky past, calmness in spirit and soul, peace to all who are weary, guilty, disturbed or burdened. He lifts the dark shadows from the mind. *Nothing is too hard for the Lord.* God has said, "I myself will tend my sheep and make them lie down. . . I will search for the lost and bring back the strays. I will bind up the injured and strengthen the weak" (Ezekiel 34:15–16).

Two men were once looking over a remote area in the Western Highlands. One man said, "What a wilderness! There's nothing on earth to be done with a wasteland like this." But the other man, a hydro-electric engineer, said, "Let me build a dam there; let me harness those waters there; and I'll give you enough power to supply half a dozen cities!" Similarly, Jesus sees the possibilities in every situation and in every man and woman. He loved people not for what they were, but more for *what they could become*. His was the eternal optimism of God.

When God saves us, all our sins are forgiven and forgotten, forever. Recently a thirteen-year-old lad was trying to find God, and peace and pardon. He went to different churches, asking questions, listening to those who had something to say, but he just could not grasp it. He thought God was a million miles away. Then, out of exasperation, he went into his garden at home and wrote down on a sheet of paper every sin he had committed, everything he could remember. It was a long list. Then he got a match and lit the piece of paper. As it burned he pointed at it and quoted a scripture he had been taught: "Christ died for my sins!" He kept repeating it as the paper burnt into ashes and was blown into nothingness by the wind. He shouted after it "Christ died for my sins!" Soon he felt that that had indeed happened. Burning the list of his sins had illustrated the truth to him, so that he could lay hold of it in reality. He felt and knew that his sins had gone! Christ had taken them right away, completely. "As far as the east is from the west, so far has he removed our transgressions from us" (Psalm 103:12). Soon he was in a lively, living fellowship of God's people.

CHANGED LIVES

A man called to see a local minister recently. The minister didn't know his visitor, but asked him in. "Now, what can I do for you?" he enquired. "Well," was the reply, "I'd like to know if I can join your church." The minister stared. "Why do you want to join *my* church?" he asked. "Well," said the visitor, "I work in a factory, and the chap at the machine next to mine used to be the meanest man I knew, as well as the laziest and the most dishonest. But since his wife got him to attend your church he's become altogether changed, and he won't rest until I come along with him. I thought I ought to ask you first, though. My workmate is a different chap nowadays. . . I'd like to be a bit more like him."

That true story is typical of what is happening in the revival today. People's lives are being radically changed by God's power.

John Paton went to the Pacific island of Tanna to proclaim the saving love of God. A tablet on the island says, "When he landed in 1848 there were no Christians here – and when he left in 1872 there were no heathens." Through Paton the Lord had changed many lives on Tanna. He was just a channel for God's boundless love.

W. E. Sangster, the well-known Methodist preacher, once remarked that "Jesus sees double." he went on to explain: "He sees us not only as the people we are, but as the people we might become. 'Thou art Simon . . . thou shalt be Peter.'" Jesus saw the potential in people.

God is calling more and more folk to change their ways and lives by his ever-available power. I know of a multitude of people from every walk of life who have been transformed by the power of Jesus. Unruly criminal teenagers, wild, uncouth Bikers and uncontrollable young women have become peaceable, contented, helpful, loving people, living to help and not mar, to rebuild and not destroy. Drunkard husbands have changed into kind, thoughtful, sober, hard-working, marvellous partners. Wives who were once unfaithful, selfish, God-rejecting and lustful are now pure, virtuous, spiritual and wholesome, reconciled to their families. These miracles are happening to the famous and rich, and to the poor and unknown. In the tough working-class estates of our big cities and in the villages of our countryside people are experiencing a mighty change in their hearts and personal lives. "Therefore, if anyone is in Christ, he is a new creation; the old has gone, the new has come!" (2 Corinthians 5:17).

3

THE REVIVAL EXALTS JESUS

"What is this Jesus to you?" one newly born Christian was asked. He replied, "Think of the best on earth, and Christ is a thousand times better!" A young man asked recently, "How can I love my Saviour more?" A difficult question! But it shows the great desire to exalt Jesus which is a characteristic of the present revival. The redeeming compassion of Christ is touching thousands; hell is being mastered, the devil defeated, sin atoned for through faith in Jesus' finished work. Many are being rescued by the glorious Saviour.

Worldly people cannot see the exalted, marvellous Christ. According to them it is foolish and crazy to trust God. I have seen such people crowd into my meetings. Their faces often show a lack of interest; many are bored before the start, restless and sometimes mocking. They are not used to sitting and listening to the Word of God. But as they hear God's eternal truths powerfully preached, as they witness astonishing miracles, as they see the mighty, living God at work, their attitude changes. They stand aghast, they shout praises to God, they run to the altar to see the miracles, they are filled with holy awe, and some even weep at the signs of God's presence. A few services later they are exalting Christ along with people who have been Christians for many years!

THE MAGNIFICENT ONE

Archbishop Cranmer referred to the "Jewels of Christ's blood, character and goodness". When he became converted, C. S. Lewis called Jesus "the Magnificent One". Every spiritual awakening brings a fresh exaltation of the Living Christ. The eager converts in the present revival are totally dedicated to Jesus; he means everything to them, every moment of the day.

Each person exalts Christ in a different way. A poet has expressed this truth well:

To the artist	He is the altogether lovely one.
To the architect	He is the chief cornerstone.
To the baker	He is the living bread.
To the banker	He is the hidden treasure.
To the doctor	He is the great physician.
To the editor	He is the good news.
To the electrician	He is the light of the world.
To the farmer	He is the Lord of the harvest.
To the geologist	He is the rock of ages.

To the horticulturist	*He is the true vine.*
To the jeweller	*He is the pearl of great price.*
To the philosopher ..	*He is the wisdom of God.*
To the printer	*He is the true type.*
To the student	*He is the incarnate truth.*
To the sinner	*He is the lamb of God which taketh away the sin of the world.*
To the true believer	*He is the Son of the Living God, the Saviour, Redeemer, very God of very God, the exalted, lovely, peerless Lord.*

Lord Tennyson remarked, "His character was even more wonderful than His miracles." Many worldly Christians cry, "Oh, look what the world has come to!" But Christ-exalting believers cry, "Look who has come to the world!" He is truly King of Kings and Lord of Lords!

ONLY ONE WAY

The BBC interviewer looked at me askance. "You mean to say, Mr Banks, that there is no allowance for any other religious teaching in your theology, that you are adamant that there is only one way to God?" This sort of question is getting more and more prevalent among media people, school teachers, sociologists and the like; they're astonished that anyone these days can be dogmatic! A few years ago I talked with some Muslims and others on ITV and told them that Christ was the only way of salvation, other religions being false. This caused a national uproar, but it brought Christ to the attention of millions of people.

These lines were found in a motel in the USA recently:

Indulgence says	*drink your way out.*
Philosophy says	*think your way out.*
Science says	*invent your way out.*
Industry says	*work your way out.*
Communism says	*strike your way out.*
Fascism says	*bluff your way out.*
Militarism says	*fight your way out.*
But Christ *says*	I am the way out.

Thousands today are "turning the corner" out of society's deep darkness and finding the One who is "the Way and the Truth and the Life".

Jesus declared, "No-one comes to the Father except *through me*" (John 14:6). Peter said, "Salvation is found in no-one else, for there is no other name under heaven given to men by which we must be saved" (Acts 4:12). So we are preaching through the land again that Jesus is the Regenerator, the Rock, the Reconciler, the Revealer, the Redeemer, the Saviour, the Shepherd, the Physician and the Purifier.

A man went forward at an evangelistic service,

and the counsellor told him to believe in Jesus. He went back the next night and talked with another counsellor, who also told him to believe in Jesus. This time the inquirer was saved. Later he met the first counsellor, who asked what the second man had said that brought him peace. The new convert replied, "He told me to believe in Jesus." The counsellor said, "But that's what I told you to do!" "That's true," said the new convert, "but you told me to *believe* in Jesus. He told me to believe in *Jesus*. I was looking at my weak faith, but he stressed faith's object. He told me to let Jesus do it all." If you focus on your faith, you will be miserable. If you look to *Jesus* you will be deeply contented.

Confucius said, "I know the way." Krishna said, "I can show you the way." Rev. Moon said, "I see the way." Mohammed said, "I am the prophet of the way." Buddha said, "I am seeking the way." The New Age Movement says, "Come, let us all travel together on the way." But Jesus said, "I *am* the way."

4

A RETURN TO THE CROSS

I was holding a fruitful mission in a minster town, famous for its abbey. I was preaching on the sufferings of Christ. An elderly lady came to me afterwards and said, "I have been a church worker in the Abbey and have heard almost every sermon preached there over the past twenty-five years, but I have never before heard anyone preach about 'the suffering Christ'."

Luther called Jesus "the crucified God". Jesus spoke of his suffering many times before Calvary. "I have a baptism to undergo" (Luke 12:50), he said, meaning his suffering on the Cross. "Without the shedding of [Jesus'] blood there is no forgiveness", wrote Paul (Hebrews 9:22); "for the joy set before him [Jesus] endured the cross, scorning its shame" (Hebrews 12:2). Gypsy Smith declared, "Sin must be strong, when it takes only the real fingers of the bleeeding, crucified hands of Christ to remove it."

Much of the modern church in Britain has forgotten the Cross. Churches have pursued all sorts of side-issues and have missed the Cross. Even some evangelicals have proclaimed a "little" cross. Many say Christ can forgive, but they don't believe that there is physical healing in the Cross and the suffering of Christ. It's amazing how God's people can be sidetracked! It is the Cross we are called to lift high. It is when Jesus is lifted up on that Cross that he draws all men unto himself. And it is when he is lifted up that miracles, signs and wonders occur.

A godly minister once wrote:

I stayed for a night at Banbury. Naturally I was interested to see Banbury Cross, which the nursery rhyme connects with the fine lady on the white horse. But Banbury has a very handsome church. I went into it in the morning before I left Banbury, and I saw a very wonderful thing. As I came in through the front door the church looked very dark, for there was no lighting. Then my eye travelled to the faraway end of the building. On the altar there was a polished brass cross and that cross was shining like a star through the dark. There was no artificial lighting on it. With its own light, that cross was shining, so that it stood out in the dark even from far away.

J. L. Hodson, in one of his war books, tells of a conversation he had with a fellow journalist on the morning after London's most devastating air raid. The journalist said to him: "Did you see the cross on St Paul's, old boy? Nobody has ever seen it shine and glow as it did that night. Clouds of smoke rolled by it, an unearthly beauty was over it."

Thank God that in these dark times, the Cross is shining through and making a powerful comeback, in these days of divine visitation. The way of the Cross is the way of redemption. "He redeemed us to God, by his blood" (Revelation 5:9). Jesus said on the Cross, "It is finished", meaning that the transaction was finished, completed, fully achieved, perfectly performed, all fulfilled, entirely done, concluded, never to be done again, never to be added to! He suffered, the sinless one, that the sinful might be made righteous through him.

Remember:

No Cross – no salvation!

No Cross – no revival!

No Cross – no resurrection and no heaven!

CHRIST CRUCIFIED

I am often asked the reason for the success of the revival. The answer is simple: we are seeing revival because *we are preaching Christ crucified*. This revival is a return to the proclamation of the Cross. We glory in nothing except the Cross of our Lord Jesus Christ. Sadly, for generations many churches have pursued one side-issue after another; they have lost sight of the heart of the Gospel, which is the Cross.

John Stott writes, "No doctrine can be called truly Christian that is not centred on the Cross." Bonhoeffer said, days before dying in a Nazi concentration camp, "Only the suffering God can save us."

The traditionalists of the church have ritualized the Cross; the liberals have rationalized the Cross; the evangelicals have marginalized the Cross; many charismatics have by-passed the Cross. Gordon Fee states, "To move beyond the Cross is not to move on at all, but is to abandon Christ altogether."

Jesus calls us out of our parochial isolation, our little huddles, our evangelical social ghettoes, to shout from the housetops the message of the Cross. The rediscovery of lively worship has led to a neglect of the vital central point of the message in many churches. Dr Coggan, former Archbishop of Canterbury, stated recently, "We have a generation of young Christians who are foreigners to this great truth of the Bible . . . the Cross."

P. T. Forsythe wrote, "Christ is to us what His Cross is. All that Christ was in heaven or on earth, I repeat, is to us, just what His Cross is. You do not understand Christ until you understand His Cross."

The message of the Cross defies all human thinking and reasoning. The miracle of Calvary is that although it happened 2,000 years ago, it has the amazing power to project its astounding grace and effect forward into countless lives today. There is astonishing power in Christ crucified. There is enough power in the offering of Calvary to cover and wipe away all human sin.

So the message of this fresh revival is based on the bedrock truth of the finished work of Calvary. What an incredible joy and privilege it is to share the glorious message of the crucified Saviour!

Paul wrote: "For what I received I passed on to you as of first importance: that Christ died for our sins according to the Scriptures, that he was buried, that he was raised on the third day" (1 Corinthians 15:3–4). In his Pentecost sermon, Peter emphasized God's purpose in the death and resurrection of Jesus: "This man was handed over to you by God's set purpose and foreknowledge; and you, with the help of wicked men, put him to death by nailing him to the cross. But God raised him from the dead" (Acts 2:23–24). Peter confirms this in his first letter (1 Peter 1:18–21), where he also sees "the sufferings of Christ and the glories that would follow" as the great theme of the Old Testament prophets (verses 10–12).

THE CORE OF THE GOSPEL

"You preach a death religion," said the man angrily. "It's all about the suffering of God!" Although he meant it as a derogatory statement, it was indeed a commendation of the vital core of the message which is increasingly coming across in the present awakening. We are seeing a return to the preaching of the Cross.

The only authentic Jesus is the one who died on the Cross. Malcolm Muggeridge, the famed converted atheist, said just before he died, "When I caught a glimpse of the Cross, my heart would suddenly stand still." We are proclaiming anew, here is no criminal going to his doom, but a King marching to his throne! Thank God, there is a new apostolic emphasis on the Cross. Its magnetic power is irresistible; it is both the answer and the key to the mysteries of sin and suffering.

Many Christians are influenced by the spirit of the age, and so they do not grasp hold of the immensity of the power released at Calvary. As Paul wrote, we are "reconciled to God through the death of his Son" (Romans 5:10). Every blessing we receive — whether it be the healing of a soul spiritually, or the healing of a diseased body physically — comes to us by virtue of the Cross. Jesus came to restore all that was lost through the fall of Adam. *God did it all.* As Archbishop Temple commented, "There is nothing we can give towards our salvation, except the sin which needs the pardon."

The great question coming to the fore in the 1990s, as in past revivals, is "Why did Christ die?"

Octavius Winslow summed it up in a neat statement: "Who delivered up Jesus to die? Not Judas
for money; not Pilate for fear; not the Jews for envy;
but *the Father, for love.*"

P. T. Forsythe wrote, "In the work of Christ in
reconciliation, the whole church rests; if you move
from this centre, the church is doomed to death."
Indeed, as Canon Peter Green wrote, "Only the man
who is prepared to own his share in the guilt of the
Cross may claim his share in its grace." Horatius
Bonar expressed it well:

'Twas I that shed the sacred blood, I nailed him
to the tree;
I crucified the Christ of God; I joined the mockery.
Of all that shouting multitude, I feel that I am one,
And in that din of voices rude, I recognize my own.
Around the Cross the throng I see, Mocking the
Sufferer's groan;
Yet still my voice it seems to be, As if I mocked
alone.

The motive of the Cross was in the heart of God,
the saving initiative originated in the Father:
"because of the mercy of our God" (Luke 1:78);
"because of his great love for us" (Ephesians 2:4);
and "because of the grace of God that brings salvation" (Titus 2:11).

John Calvin wrote: "In the Cross of Christ, the

incomparable goodness of God is set before the whole world. The glory of God ... shines never more brightly than in the Cross." We see the uniqueness of Christ's sacrifice here. "God loved us and sent his Son to be the propitiation for our sins" (1 John 4:10). "God made him to be sin for us, that we might be made the righteousness of God" (2 Corinthians 5:21). Again it tells us, "God presented him as a sacrifice through faith in his blood" (Romans 3:25).

Karl Barth declared: "God's own heart suffered on the Cross." Archbishop Cranmer said, "This is the strong rock and foundation of the Christian religion." P. T. Forsythe said, "God dying for man ... and for such men ... hostile, malignantly hostile men ... the one thing God could not do in the face of such human rebellion, was nothing; he must either inflict punishment, or assume it. And he chose the latter course, as honouring the law, while saving the guilty. He took his own judgement."

Here is the decisive victory of the Lamb of God. We truly see what God is like. No wonder Charles Wesley wrote:

Amazing love, How can it be,
That Thou, my God, should'st die for me!

You and I nailed Jesus to the tree; he went because of our sins. Christ's death is substitutionary. His sacrifice turns away the anger of God. John Stott wrote:

I could never myself believe in God, if it were not for the cross. The only God I believe in is the One Nietzsche ridiculed as "God on the cross". In the real world of pain, how could one worship a God who was immune to it? I have entered many Buddhist temples in different Asian countries and stood respectfully before the statue of the Buddha, his legs crossed, arms folded, eyes closed, the ghost of a smile playing round his mouth, a remote look on his face, detached from the agonies of the world. But each time after a while I have had to turn away. And in imagination I have turned instead to that lonely, twisted, tortured figure on the cross, nails through hands and feet, back lacerated, limbs wrenched, brow bleeding from thorn-picks, mouth dry and intolerably thirsty, plunged in God-forsaken darkness. This is the God for me! He laid aside his immunity to pain. He entered our world of flesh and blood, tears and death. He suffered for us. Our sufferings become more manageable in the light of his. There is still a question mark against human suffering, but over it we boldly stamp another mark, the cross which symbolizes divine suffering. The cross of Christ . . . is God's only self-justification in such a world as ours.

As we uplift the Cross, twisted lives are straightened, lives marred by sin are made anew. As we uplift the Cross, and believe it, our souls are purged from transgression, guilt, darkness and fear. Edward Shillito, shattered by the carnage of the First World War, found comfort in the fact that Jesus was able to show his disciples the scars of his crucifixion. It inspired him to write his poem *Jesus of the Scars*:

If we have never sought, we seek thee now;
Thine eyes burn through the dark, our only stars.
We must have sight of thorn-marks on thy brow;
We must have thee, O Jesus of the scars.
The other gods were strong, but thou wast weak;
They rode, but thou didst stumble to a throne;
But to our wounds only God's wounds can speak,
And not a god has wounds, but thou alone.

Let us not be offended by the stigma of the Cross. Today we are seeing a return to the emphasis of the Cross – thank God! The stigmata of Jesus, in the spirit if not in the body, remain a mark of authentication for every Christian disciple, and especially for every Christian witness.

Said Thomas, "Except I shall see in his hands the print of the nails. . . I will not believe." Dr Parker of London said that what Thomas said of Christ, the world is saying about the church. And the world is also saying to every preacher: "Unless I see in your hands the print of the nails, I will not believe."

OFFENSIVE BUT EFFECTIVE

Many unbelievers say to me, "This is a sick joke about God caring; if he does, why doesn't he do something about the mess the world is in? Let God prove himself! Why doesn't he stop the children dying of starvation in Bosnia, or wipe out the evil IRA terrorists in Northern Ireland, or heal the mother about to die of cancer, leaving four tiny children? It's all so unfair! If God truly loves, let him do these things, and I will believe on him."

But it is because *he died on the Cross* that we are saved from our sins; it is because he stayed on the Cross that we have comfort, peace, healing and hope in all these hopeless situations.

The Cross defies man's understanding; the Word says, "The natural man receiveth not the things of God." The Cross is still mocked. The Muslims recently held a rally at the Albert Hall; the title of the lecture was "Christ's Crucifixion or Crucifiction?" The blood of the atonement is anathema to them; it is weakness, folly; it is impossible, they say, for Almighty God to die! But Paul said, "To those whom God has called, Christ is the power of God and the wisdom of God" (1 Corinthians 1:24); and again, "The foolishness of God is wiser than man's wisdom, and the weakness of God is stronger than man's strength" (1 Corinthians 1:25).

Some people walk out of our Revival Rallies when I make much of the Cross. One Australian preacher said I ought to preach something "more charismatic". An English preacher once said to me, "You will be out of a job in another two years. No one will want you preaching *that* all the time!" Since that remark was made ten years ago, I have preached almost every day of the year for ten years. *People are flocking to hear the preaching of the Cross like never before.*

Gorden Fee wrote: "In the Cross, God outsmarted his human creatures and thereby nullified their wisdom; he also 'overpowered' his enemies, with lavish grace and forgiveness, and thereby divested them of strength." The Christian message of the Cross defies all human thinking and reasoning. It demands not our understanding but our faith.

This is the message which God has called us to proclaim – a message which centres on the Cross, a message which is inescapably offensive, yet a message which is powerfully effective in the hearts of those who believe. The church at Corinth could bear testimony to its transforming power. For before their conversion, they had been a pretty unsavoury bunch. They had included "the sexually immoral, adulterers, male prostitutes, homosexual offenders, thieves, drunkards, slanderers, swindlers"

(1 Corinthians 6:9). But this dissolute group had experienced the transforming power of the Cross in their lives: they had been "washed . . . sanctified . . . justified in the name of the Lord Jesus Christ and by the Spirit of God" (1 Corinthians 6:11). The Christian message is powerfully effective. There is, however, nothing automatic about the Cross. Faith is necessary to link us with it.

We can point to the evidence of the Gospel's transforming power in our own lives and in the lives of thousands coming to Christ in the current revival in many parts of Britain.

5

SHARING THE GOOD NEWS

I recently led a crusade in one of the toughest parts of Bristol – St Werburgh. All the churches in the area were closed, there were several Buddhist groups, and there were only four or five dedicated Christians. The Christians held fourteen prayer meetings a week! God moved. In that hellish place of utter darkness, with desperate, longing, thirsty people who knew nothing of Christ in every home and street, God broke through. Crowds came to the crusade and many people were saved and healed. The Buddhists chanted against us, but they soon fled when a woman who was pushed into the meeting in a wheelchair walked out unaided! We have a growing church there today. Light, hope and revival have come to that hell on earth!

Suddenly God breaks in on people as we go and tell them the Good News – this is the thrill of revival! Who will carry the Word to the darkest hell? God is looking for men and women who will go all the way with him. We must press the message home. *For precious souls nothing is too much*. This is the new attitude growing in the revival.

After the fourth-century Battle of Adrianople, Ambrose, bishop of Milan, spent all his money to ransom the Roman soldiers who had been captured by the Goths in battle. He even melted down sacred vessels to turn them into money. When he was accused of sacrilege, he replied that the souls for whom the Lord had shed his blood were more precious than vessels. We must sacrifice all for lost souls.

The Gospel changes lives here and now and for eternity. Don't be ashamed of the Gospel, for "it is the power of God for the salvation of everyone who believes" (Romans 1:16).

Whatever our place in the Body of Christ, let's actively and prayerfully invite others into God's Kingdom. After all, God doesn't have a plan A, a plan B and a plan C for evangelizing the world. He has only one plan, and that's *you and me*.

William Barclay used to tell the story of a man who lived in a tenement in a respectable artisan district in a certain great city. This man wanted to know about Christ. He began to go to a church which was near at hand. In that church about the first person he met was the man who lived in the flat across the landing from his own home. That man was an elder in the church, and never in years had he mentioned the church to his next door neighbour, and never had he made any attempt to guide him or lead him or persuade him into it. What a failure! Christians ought to be missionaries. If they aren't, they are failures. Start by evangelizing the people around you. We must bear our part of the sacred duty to spread and share the Good News.

In his long life, Sir Winston Churchill wrote and said a great many things worth remembering, and one of the wittiest and wisest of all his remarks was surely, "We are all worms, but I think I am a glow-worm." You and I may agree that we live in a dark world, and we may even humble ourselves enough to acknowledge that we are nobody very much . . . but even if we are worms, let's be glow-worms, and light the darkness just a bit!

The challenge is to press for the highest and best in God and never be satisfied with second-best or half measures. A prophetic people will never be afraid to challenge the works of evil or the perpetrators of evil.

A Third-World bishop said of the Gospel, "It is like manna — it cannot be kept. If we do not share it, we lose it. If we do not use it, it goes stale. It has been given to us like bread for our daily use."

After a church service, a businessman surprised the preacher by saying, "If you were a salesman of mine, I'd sack you." He went on to say, "You got my attention by your appearance, voice and manner; your logical discourse aroused my interest;

you warmed my heart, and then you stopped without asking me to do anything about it. In business the important thing is to get people to sign on the dotted line." *We must challenge people about Jesus*.

People want to hear from God. They need comfort, power and freedom from their guilt, slavery and despair. *People are at rock bottom*; they are desperate. We must lift them, save them and bring them to a choice.

A workman was busy breaking up large paving stones into smaller irregular pieces. The local minister came by and commented on the hard work the man was doing. The workman smiled, then said, "You know, minister, these stones are like the ten commandments – you can go on breaking them, but you can never get rid of them!" Yes, people can go on breaking the commandments, but they can never get away from the weight on their conscience. God's commands are forever, a challenge always. People will live and die in the dark, to be judged by them, if they do not receive light, reconciliation, eradication of guilt, forgiveness from God.

This is God's Day – revival is coming to the ordinary people, as we go and show them the magnificent God, and the great reality of Jesus, and the wonderful sight of the sons of God coming into their own life-changing liberty.

HARVEST-TIME HAS COME

For far too long only a trickle of folk have been coming out of the church on a Sunday evening, while across the road the crowds pour from the nightclubs, pubs and bingo halls. But now a new spirit is abroad. The Lord is saying to his people, "Arise, come away, the winter is past" (Song of Solomon 2:10). Harvest-time has come.

Asked about the secret of his great success in conquering the world, Alexander the Great replied, "I acted time after time without delay." *We must not wait; now is the time to strike for God!* We must go where the people are. It takes the mighty power of the Holy Spirit to break us free from the bondage of procrastination and non-urgency that has gripped Christians in the nation in recent years.

It is harvesting hour! God is now disturbing and discomforting us. He is calling us to go forth with the thrilling, exciting message of Christ.

One day a mother called her little girl down from her bedroom to come and have tea, but the faint reply was, "I'm coming." Later there was no sign of her, so the mother called again, "Come down for tea." There was still no appearance, only a disinterested "I'm coming, Mummy." Finally Mum went to the bottom of the stairs and shouted, "Stop coming and come!" Our delayed obediences are a great hindrance to God's blessing and doing greater wonders with us. We must obey, we must come, we must go forth with him and take the good tidings to sinful mankind. The tragic destination of those who walk in darkness is almost too sad to contemplate. So gather the harvest with us now, and be enthralled with incalculable blessings.

As C. S. Swindoll put it, "Life is like a coin. You can spend it any way you like, but you can only spend it once." Spend your life for God. Reap the harvest! C. S. Lewis wrote, "This world is enemy-occupied territory – the rightful King [Jesus] has landed in disguise, and is calling us all to a great campaign."

EVANGELISM IS OUR RESPONSIBILITY

Man is ready for the Gospel at this hour. He is under deep distress, his worldly appetites and lusts are fading, he needs a Saviour. There is today a growing interest in the Gospel. But many Christians are doing nothing to spread the Good News. Many believers are having a comfortable time in their cosy fellowships. One lady, who had gone from house church to house church, was asked by my wife how she was getting on. She replied, "Oh, this new house group is marvellous. We have lovely times of blessing, liberty and freedom – it's fantastic!" But when Lilian asked her how many souls she had won for Jesus, she tried to change the subject. Asked what evangelism they did as individuals or as a group, she again changed the subject, as if the question were not important. All she cared about was having her own spiritual needs met. This attitude is very dangerous. It may be renewal, but it's not revival.

Does it worry you if people are without hope? Do you care for souls without Christ? Can you sleep easily at night, knowing that millions are going into conscious eternal hell without any Saviour? Many, many Christians seem to have lost interest in the lost, or never had any interest in the first place. The old verse asks us, "Could a mariner sit idle if he heard a drowning cry? Could a doctor sit in comfort and just let his patients die? Could a fireman sit idle, let men burn and give no hand? Can you sit at ease in Zion with the world around you damned?"

Fred Somebody, Tom Everybody, Peter Anybody and Joe Nobody were neighbours. All four belonged to the same church. Everybody went fishing on the Lord's day, or stayed at home to watch television. Anybody could have gone to church regularly, but he was afraid Somebody wouldn't speak to him, so guess who went along – Nobody.

Nobody was the only decent one of the four. Nobody did the visitation. Nobody welcomed strangers at the door. Once they needed a Sunday School teacher. Everybody thought Anybody would do it, and Anybody thought Somebody would do

it, and can you guess who did it? That's right –
Nobody.

It happened that a fifth neighbour who was not
a Christian moved into the area. Everybody thought
Somebody should try to win him for Christ. Anybody could have made the effort. You probably
know who finally won him – Nobody.

Don't be a Nobody. Don't let the blood of sinners
be on your hands in eternity.

It is our responsibility how much of the harvest
we get at this mighty time, how much of the Holy
Spirit we avail ourselves of, how much we grab and
take of this inheritance of God. God is seeking to
give, to impart, to flood us with untold blessings.
We must seek him. *It is up to us*. Are you getting
your inheritance? Are you in the revival?

A few years ago a book called *Seekers after God*
was published in the USA. It sold out in many cities.
An exasperated bookshop manager telegraphed the
wholesalers, but back came the reply, "No *Seekers
after God* in Philadelphia, Washington, Los Angeles
or Denver." No seekers after God – how sad. Are
you a seeker? It's the seekers who are getting the
most from the revival. God is longing to give and
give; he wants to bless you with his Word and his
revival. If you seek him too, you will find all that
he has for you. But many believers are half-hearted,
apathetic, unbelieving, settled down, cautious; they
have stopped seeking, asking and receiving.

ASHAMED OF CHRIST?

I was once asked to speak at a meeting in a large government building in London where thousands were employed. The leader of the weekly Christian Union meeting told me he was convinced that at least a few hundred Christians worked there. "But," he said, "they won't take a public stand for Christ." Were they ashamed? Yes, I think so. How terrible to be ashamed of Christ, who loved us and died to save us from our sins. Our Lord made it very clear what would happen to those who are ashamed of him and deny him: "If anyone publicly acknowledges me as his friend, I will openly acknowledge him as my friend before my Father in heaven. But if anyone publicly denies me I will openly deny him before my Father in heaven" (Matthew 10:32–33). Paul was certainly never ashamed of Christ, as the many exciting accounts of his witnessing for Christ in the Book of Acts clearly tell us. Paul knew the Gospel was a life-giving message. It gripped him, he was thrilled with Jesus, he lived in the reality of it.

It's thrilling to see young believers in this revival go out at night on to the streets of Gloucester, Bristol and other cities to share the Good News of Christ and to give soup and sandwiches to the homeless. They are bringing the reality of the Gospel of Christ to the poor.

We must give all, that all may hear of Jesus.

Everyone who knows Jesus must tell everyone who
doesn't know him. Our hearts must be open to share
with all the radiant, living love of Christ.

One of our workers in Inverness gave an invi-
tation to one of my meetings to a Muslim man. As
soon as he read of the miracles he said, "I must go
to that meeting." He went, and he and his whole
family of five found Christ. They were visited and
linked with a local church and are now following
Jesus. This happened because someone went to
share the Gospel with them.

There is a legend that Pilate's wife was standing
by the Cross on the afternoon of the crucifixion of
Christ. She turned to the centurion and said, "Do
you think Jesus is dead?"

"No, lady, I don't," was the answer.

"Then where is he?"

"Let loose in the world, lady, where neither
Roman nor Jew nor any other man can stop the
victory of his risen life."

So God's people are today being let loose in his
power, to show the United Kingdom that God is
still on the throne, and that Jesus is alive. Millions
are deeply interested, longing for a living reality of
faith. Revival means sharing Christ with these lost
neighbours, associates, strangers, contacts and
locals.

A man found a lad crying at a railway station.
He discovered that the boy had lost his ticket and

the official would not let him on without paying, and he had no money. The man purchased a ticket for him, but made him promise that one day he would do a similar good turn for someone else. The boy agreed and got his fare home, and as the train moved away from the platform, the lad, leaning out of the window and waving the ticket, shouted to the kind gentleman, "I will pass it on, sir, I promise I will pass it on!" Revival is to pass on the glorious Good News – to pass on God's love, to pass on his care and compassion.

6

THE SERIOUSNESS OF SIN

Here is a story I heard recently. After Jesus had ascended into heaven, he was asked what would happen to his Kingdom now that he was no longer on earth. "I have left behind me eleven men," he said. "I spent three years with them, they know my teaching and my ways and they will carry on my work." "And what if they fail?" persisted the questioner. "They must not fail," replied Jesus. "I have no others." So, because those first disciples were faithful to their task and spread the Good News to others, who in their turn did the same, Christianity grew, and 2,000 years later it has reached every corner of the earth. It's a thought to inspire us.

What a tremendous mission has been given to us who believe in his Name! What a great and exalted task! What a challenge from an Almighty God to our generation! He did not spare even his own Son, but surrendered him for the salvation and deliverance of all who believe. But Paul says in Romans 10:14, "How then shall they call on him in whom

they have not believed? And how shall they believe
in him of whom they have not heard? And how
shall they hear without a preacher? And how shall
they preach, except they be sent?" How many
people are going to be saved if we stay sitting at
home, shutting up our hearts against our fellow
men? Millions of people are perishing! Why? There
is no one who preaches the Gospel to them! Because
faith comes by the hearing of the Word of God. The
people have to hear who Jesus is.

Oh, I can hear the slave chains rattling in my
ears. The slaves are on their way, trudging forward.
There are millions of them. Their faces are tense.
The chains are heavy and strong. They are trying to
appear happy, but it is just a mask. God has shown
us the reality of daily life in the world. He has
shown us the slaves of sin, the slaves of drink, the
slaves of unclean powers from hell, the slaves of
addictive drugs, the slaves of homosexuality.

There are two powers at work in the world: the
power of good and the power of evil. The Gospel
of John says the power of evil is the devil. He comes
only to kill, steal and destroy. But the power of
good – that is, Jesus – has come to give us life and
life more abundantly. In the Bible I read how great
sinners such as prostitutes, robbers, murderers and
thieves who were living deep in sin found salvation
and deliverance through faith in God and his Son,
Jesus Christ. Their lives were totally changed.

The God of the Bible has not changed. His love
has not changed. His power is still exactly the same.
And the wonderful thing about it is that what God
does for others, he will do for you too, if you will
only listen, if you will only believe. If you will only
do what the Bible says, God is always ready to fulfil
his promises. God wants to deliver you from every
chain of sin, and he wants to save your soul and
forgive your sins.

Many Christians are far removed from the
world's needs. They don't know what it is like to
be in the devil's prison, they have been so respectable for so long. Other Christians have just got used
to the sin all around them. They no longer bat an
eyelid at man's depravity, hurt, wounds and cries
for help. They accept the status quo as it is; they
have given up trying to change it!

DEEP CONVICTION

We must show unsaved people the depth of their
darkness, the seriousness of sin, the heavy weight
of guilt. In the revival sin is being shown once more
for what it is. There is deep conviction of transgressions. People are at last seeing that the cause of
their spiritual sickness is their dreadful sinfulness.
Sin is a serious hostility to God. It is a defiance, an
aggression, an arrogance towards their Maker. It is
an assertion of human independence from the Lord.

You cannot dress a wound which is

For too long the church in the United Kingdom has, in Jeremiah's words, "dressed the wounds of my people as though it were not serious" (Jeremiah 6:14). This lesson is coming out of the revival: God takes man most seriously, and he takes sin seriously too!

In this revival the anxious, the drugged, the sexually permissive, the weak, the burdened, the desperate and the sick are flocking to the glorious Gospel feast of the ages. The lame, the blind and the halt are being called from the highways and the hedges to discover our precious, wonderful Jesus.

I hear him calling above the noise of the chains of sin, by which the sinners are bound. I hear the voice of him who hung there on the Cross of Calvary. Do you hear it too, friend? Listen carefully to what he has to say. He is calling out, "It is finished! It is finished!" What has he finished? He, who was without sin, hung there in the place of sinners and paid the penalty for their sins. This is the core of the revival message, and it is the answer to the seriousness of sin!

IN A HURRY WITH THE GOSPEL

"What's the rush? Let me go home and think about it." In spite of the staggering things happening in the revival, I still hear remarks like this being said. The man who voiced those words was never seen by me again. Another person said, "Maybe in a few years' time I will commit myself." That person is dead now! People think they can take their time over making a commitment to Jesus, but their time may be short. God wants us to become Christians *now*, without delay, but the devil says, "No need to hurry."

A man had a dream. Satan was holding a meeting for all the wicked spirits, and he said, "Who will go forth to ruin souls?" A hand went up. "And what will you tell them that will ruin them?"

The reply was, "There is no need to worry about religious things, for there is no God."

Satan replied, "That answer is no good, because everyone knows there is a God."

Another hand went up and his approach was "I'll tell them that there is a God, but he doesn't care what happens to those who are little and insignificant compared with him."

Satan said, "No use, they know he loves them."

A third response was, "I'll go and tell them there is a God, he loves them and wants them to come to him, but there is plenty of time, no need to hurry, they can put it off."

Satan told the spirit to go and do his evil work.

The man awoke – was it only a dream?

I fear for churches who say we are going too fast in revival: slow little housegroups who crawl at a snail's pace; fellowships who have no passion to get

those who crawl at a snail's pace

on with the job of communicating the Gospel to the mass of sinners who are driving to hell at breakneck speeds.

We must hurry with the Good News of Christ. God wants to show people that he is alive in the United Kingdom. The God of the New Testament – the God of miracles – is in a hurry to save and to grasp men and women from the burning. As Tom Fuller used to say, "It's never too soon to repent, but it may soon be too late." That is why we are in a hurry with the glorious Good News today.

7

REVIVAL THROUGH THE WORD

In the present revival the Word of God is changing thousands. People are leaving the bingo halls, the dance halls and pubs, the nightclubs and their wordly pleasures, to *take up the Bible again*, and to read and love it. I gave away a hundred Bibles one night in Devon recently at the end of a crowded revival meeting. Most of those who received them had never owned a Bible before and promised to read a chapter a day. We sell more Bibles than any other book. In one place someone composed this verse:

The devil trembles in his knees,
when Bibles are sold as cheap as these!

The Acts of the Apostles keeps saying: "The Word of God grew and multiplied." No other kind of growth will do, no matter by what wisdom or efficiency. Seminars, business principles, tongues, prophecy, music, personality and publicity all have their place, but they should not replace the Bible. First and foremost the church is *for* the Word. Christians are Word-produced.

By the Word we can change the world, we can save the world, we can beat our problems. TV producers have said to me again and again, "It's so hard to get over to your fellow ministers who come into these studios that they are not talking to their own constituency. The masses out there do not understand your Christian jargon. You must use everyday, communicative words." Sadly, many believers are out of step, lost in their own little world.

Whatever success I have had during my thirty-eight-year ministry of soul-winning and church planting I attribute to my *constant emphasis on the divine Word of God*. The nation is hungry for that Word.

In a newspaper article Damian Thompson described Britain as one of the world's most secular societies, "a consequence not just of greedy materialism, but of the extraordinary feebleness of the British Churches. Even the Methodists, once Britain's most energetic evangelists, have shrunk to a middle-class pressure group." Only the real Gospel can save. The motto of this revival is becoming, "All the Word of God for all the people of God." We want all the nation to become the people of God through his Word.

A young Christian about to set off to a holiday conference was busily packing his bag. "Are you nearly ready?" called his mother. "Yes, I won't be long," he answered. "I have just to pack a guide book, a mirror, a lamp, a telescope, a microscope, some history and poetry books, a bundle of old letters, a sword, a hammer and a suit of armour." And he placed his Bible in his case and closed the lid. With the Word we have all our equipment and tools to do God's work, and *we must hurry* with the message across the whole land.

A BIBLE STUDY IN A PUB!

Recently I visited the village of Hambledon in the heart of rural Hampshire. I met crowds of young folk there. Many had been converted through the local publican's son, who was holding Bible studies in the back of the pub. Youngsters were crowding in and being changed by the Word of God.

This is typical of what is happening in the revival now. Most youngsters these days know nothing about the Bible, but in the centres of revival the basics of the Christian faith are being learned by eager young minds in school halls, community centres, university residences, house meetings and even pubs! Many of the older generation of Christians have lost their appetite for the living Word of God, but many fresh young converts are giving all their allegiance to it. We need a return to biblical preaching and teaching. Has lively worship in the past caused many to miss the importance of strong biblical teaching?

Good preaching is only ever the product of great study. Paul's letters show that Apollos and Aquila diligently studied the Word. They touched and blessed the early church and helped to establish people in the faith. Among the reasons for the lack of great preachers today is the fact that there are so few painstaking students.

When a few believers take God's Word seriously, you can have a revival on your hands. John Nicholson had promised his mother before she died that he would read her Bible every day. In 1898 he shared a hotel room with another traveller, Samuel Hill. Together they talked and prayed, and soon the Gideons were born. Now, almost a century later, one million copies of the Bible are presented in over 130 countries every two weeks. Praise the Lord for what he can do when people get fired up by the Word.

I was on ITV a short time ago, accompanied by a man named Stan Skedge. Two years before he was so crippled that he had to crawl upstairs on his knees. He had rarely read the Bible. His wife persuaded him to come to the service which I was leading at Mount Zion Church in Norwich. The Lord healed him; he went home and ran up and down the stairs, and since then he has had a new spiritual interest in God. On the live ITV programme, watched by 100,000 people, he said he had read the whole Bible through in a year.

Prayerful Bible study is vital to increase our understanding of our Christian faith and to deepen our new life in Christ. Nothing can be more important or profitable. It takes discipline. We need more than just a few minutes, with an eye on the clock, before rushing out to work. Something else has to get set aside quite deliberately to make more adequate time. It is worth spending less time listening to the conflicting voices of the world – whether the printed page, the radio or the TV – to spend more time hearing the authoritative yet loving voice of your heavenly Father.

GET INTO THE WORD

In the Bible we meet the minds of Moses and Isaiah, of John and Paul, and what minds they are! Above all this, however, in the Bible we encounter the mind of God. Through the many inspired writers we hear his voice. What a privilege it is to know God through his Word! Read with expectant faith and with openness and obedience. If you are his child, you can look to your Father to teach you what life means and how to live it. So open your whole being to God's Word. Listen to its instruction, follow its arguments, see its pictures in your imagination, experience the emotional impact of its great stories. Live in the world of the first readers of the Book; hear the Word of God as they heard it. You can then seek through God's Spirit to see how this Word applies in the 1990s and in your own life today.

I know one old lady who has read the Bible twenty-one times, and she has enjoyed every minute of it. It is the first thing she reaches for in the morning and the last thing she puts down before turning off the light at night. No wonder she is such a pleasing, peaceful, sweet character. I know that much of the restlessness that plagues the world today would disappear if more of us were like her. Whenever Jesus is Lord and rules a person, that person is living evidence of the presence and power of his Word.

Get into the Word. You may not understand a lot of it for a long time, but some of it will come clear to you soon. I am still learning a lot after nearly forty years studying it. Most of us, if we are honest with ourselves, have to admit that there are some parts of the Bible which we find hard to comprehend or accept. A lady with just such a problem once found herself at a dinner sitting next to Dr Joseph Parker, an outstanding preacher of the nineteenth century. So she aired her difficulties with him. They happened to be eating fish at the time, and Dr Parker asked her, "What do you do with the bones in your fish?" "Why, I leave them on the edge of my plate," was the surprised reply. "Well, do the same with the Bible," said Parker. "Eat the fish, and leave the bones." Wise words from a great man.

Eat all you can, take in what you can. God will help you. What you don't understand, leave until later. God is happy with that. And the more you dig into the Bible's riches, the more Christlike you will become. The Word is the foundation of the revival.

Many people, even Christians, seldom open the Bible to read it, to meditate on it, to study it. And because they fail to partake of the "milk" and "meat" of the Word, they are spiritually under-nourished. If someone were to hide your Bible, how long would it take before you missed it? One of the marks of a well-fed soul is a well-read Bible. "Do not let this Book of the Law depart from your mouth; meditate on it day and night" (Joshua 1:8).

In order for our body to receive nourishment, the food we eat must be properly digested. This process starts with chewing. The same is true of our intake of spiritual food – the Word of God. We must digest its truth in a deliberate, methodical way. Cud-chewing animals like sheep and cattle provide a fitting analogy for understanding this process. I'm sure many of us have seen a cow in the pasture under the shade of an oak tree, engaged in slow, methodical munching. The cow is ruminating. This means she chews her food, stores it in a special stomach, and then brings it back to chew again. That's how the cow derives the utmost benefit from the food. As we read the Bible and meditate on its truths, the Holy Spirit makes us aware of our sin, assures us of God's forgiveness, renews our hope, directs our steps, and gives us courage to face the spiritual battles that lie before us. A Christian needs to "chew" the Word of God every day.

For getting to know God, and the "buttress" of revival, depends on our intake of God's sayings. We must *hear* God's Word, *read* God's Word, *memorize* God's Word, *study* God's Word, *write* God's Word, *sing* God's Word, *talk* God's Word, and the *most rewarding*, *meditate* in God's Word. The poet said: "Other books are written for our information; the Bible for our *transformation*."

No wonder Charles Dickens said of Holy Scripture: "It is the best book that ever was, and ever shall be written!"

8

THE GLORY AND WONDER OF GOD

In the church in recent decades there has been far too much emphasis on man, on his image and works. This frail, fleshly view of the church has left many ministries and congregations *powerless*. One of the most encouraging aspects of the revival is the reversal of this trend. Personalities are hidden, big names have receded, leaders, singers and musicians are no longer put on a pedestal. At some fellowships I preach at, I don't even know who the pastor is until the end of the service! Increasingly all the attention is being given to Jesus himself; the meetings are charged with unrestrained love for God above. *He is being glorified*. It's marvellous!

I am told that Benedictine monks wear the insignia "IOGD" (*In Omnibus Glorificatur Deus*), which means, "In everything God glorified". What a text to emblazon on our hearts and to live out in our lives!

François Fenelon was the court preacher for King Louis XIV of France. One Sunday, when the king and his attendants arrived at the chapel for the regular service, no one else was there but the preacher. King Louis demanded, "What does this mean?" Fenelon replied, "I had published that you would not come to church today, in order that Your Majesty might see who serves God in truth and who flatters the king."

A growing church was making construction plans. In honour of the pastor's many years of ministry, the building committee told him they wanted to put his name on the cornerstone. He thanked them for their thoughtfulness, but then quoted 1 Corinthians 10:31: "Whatever you do, do all to the glory of God." He then asked that the committee not let his name appear. If you drive by that church today, instead of the pastor's name you will read these words on the cornerstone: "For the glory of God".

A little exercise I have started to give church workers in this revival is to ask them to write down in their own words "How I plan to live for the glory of God today".

Unthankfulness is a grave sin. We must not fail to give all the glory to God. The word "glory" is used 400 times in Scripture. It calls God "the Father of Glory" (Ephesians 1:7), "the Spirit of Glory" (1 Peter 4:14) and "the God of Glory" (Acts 7:2).

I like R. Hanby's words of long ago:

Who is he . . . at whose feet the shepherds fall?

Who is he in deep distress, fasting in the
wilderness?
Who is he that from the grave comes to heal and
to save?
'Tis the Lord, the King of Glory!

GIVING GLORY TO GOD

We are changing Britain because a vital part of our
lives is taken up with giving glory to our God.
Fellowships, churches and prayer groups are changing as they see that there is no revival without restoring glory to our Father!

If we are not winning souls, we are not giving
him the glory.

If we are not controlling our tongues and speaking kind, prayerful, biblical, positive, faithful words,
instead of gossip, scandal and doubt, then we are
not giving him the glory.

If we do not have a pure, holy, clean heart, then
we are not giving him the glory.

If we are not bringing our tithes into God's store-
house for the ministries he has raised up, then we
are not giving him the glory.

If we have not confessed our sins, if we do not
love our brothers and sisters, then we are not giving
him the glory.

He has given us all things, he has made us new
creations, he has given us the control of the whole

earth, he has put his glorious peace into "earthen vessels". With Billy Bray, the old Cornish evangelist, we shout, "Glory, glory, glory, glory to God!"

WONDER REDISCOVERED

At one memorable revival meeting in an auditorium in an historic English town the singing, the worship, the wonder of God and the miraculous healings moved the audience so much that their joy was audible in the theatre next door, where the people were watching a performance of *Showboat*. The noise was so loud that all the pleasure-lovers heard it, and they began to clap and applaud. That night the theatre-goers were touched by a sense of the wonder of God.

Gipsy Smith, the outstanding evangelist, always kept his freshness and joy and his ability to communicate to a needy society. Asked about his vigour at eighty-seven years of age, he replied, "I have never lost the wonder."

I jump out of bed in the mornings and shout the praises of God as my first waking words. A while ago I spent the night in the home of a Christian family. I had had a late night praying for sick people. At about 7.00 a.m. my host kindly brought my breakfast in on a tray while I was still asleep. Then I awoke and jumped up with my usual greeting to the day, oblivious of anyone in the room. I shouted loudly, "Praise the Lord! Praise the Lord for a new day!" The startled gentleman suddenly dropped the tray, and it crashed to the floor – the milk spilled all over the eggs and bacon, the tea soaked the toast, the tomato juice covered the tray. My friend smiled and said as he recovered, "Do you always wake up like that?" Embarrassed, I replied, "Always," and gave him another "Praise the Lord!" He went out of the room, roaring with laughter.

After nearly forty years since my conversion, I have never lost the joy, the wonder; every new day is exciting and filled with God's goodness and delight.

"Wonder" is a real Bible word, used some 200 times in Scripture. David said, "I will speak of thy majesty and thy wondrous works", and again, "Who is like unto thee, O Lord, doing wonders?" Many believers appreciate the wonder of God but never appropriate it. Many have lost this sense of awe and wonder.

On a train journey a man kept staring out of the window, standing up and pointing out the most simple of things, and loving and appreciating everything and chatting about it all. Someone asked him why, on such a dull journey, did he enjoy it all so immensely? He replied, "Until a few days ago I was blind, but my sight was restored after years in darkness. This is not dull, but out of this world – it's wonderful!"

The new converts and the restored believers feel

that way about God: they are thrilled, enthusiastic with reverence, full of awe and sacred wonder. I cry to God often for a fresh anointing, to see him in his glory, to hold that wonder of the Lord.

Fight the ordinariness of Western Christian living; don't slump into slow, cold-hearted, modern Christian life. Argue against the gloom. Let Spirit-filled thinking replace carnal thinking. Let him restore the glory to you. Remember that no opposition can crush the man who is filled with God's wonder. No one can disinherit such a believer. As Paul wrote, "Who shall separate us from the love of God?"

A believer full of wonder draws other souls close to God, to worship, to the Word of God. We can sing with rapturous joy, "I was once in darkness, now my eyes can see; I was lost but Jesus sought and found me. O what love he offers, O what peace he gives!"

Rudyard Kipling's prayer went, "Teach me, O Lord, to delight in simple things." Charles Kingsley, author of bestsellers like *Westward Ho!* and *The Water Babies* and also a country parson, said, "The men I have seen succeed best in life, have always been the cheerful, and men of hope and wonder." It is good to keep a healthy sense of spiritual wonder.

The text on the wall of Mount Zion Church in Norwich reads, "From the rising of the sun unto the going down of the same, the Lord's name is to be praised." This is a church where many, many

people have experienced a miracle. Folk go there
regularly, healthy and well, praising God, who were
once in wheelchairs, unable to walk upstairs,
deaf, crippled; and many who never knew Christ
have been caught up in the moving of God's Spirit,
and are new creatures in Christ. They are a thankful,
praising people of wonder who know their God.

Williard L. Sperry tells of an American student
he knew who was planning a cycle tour of England.
Dr Sperry found him poring over maps, working
out a route which would enable him to keep to
fairly level roads and avoid the hills. But what a
way to see England! He would miss Devon and
Cornwall, the Lake District, the downs and moors,
and much more beside. And if he extended his tour
to Scotland and Wales, he would see very little
indeed. How much we miss in life if we are always
seeking to "avoid the hills", to take the easy way.
We don't see the wonder of God if we stay on flat
terrain!

I heard recently of someone who read through
the New Testament armed with a red pen and a
black pen. With the black pen he underlined all the
passages to do with sorrow, weeping, pain and
death. With the red one, he marked the words deal-
ing with joy, singing, laughter, feasting and the like.
He said that when he then flipped over the pages of
his New Testament, it seemed to be dominated by
red underlining. Where did this idea that Christ-

ianity is a gloomy business come from? The Bible is happy news for us all. It is a book of faith, of wonder, of wonderful things. Thomas Carlyle, the great nineteenth-century Scottish writer, said, "Wonder is the basis of worship."

TEN THOUSAND WONDERS

A teacher had been talking to his class about the Seven Wonders of the World – the Pyramids of Egypt, the Hanging Gardens of Babylon, the Temple of Diana at Ephesus and so on. Towards the end of the lesson, the teacher asked his pupils to compile a list of what they considered to be the Seven Wonders of the Modern World, for technology has given us some pretty amazing things. After they had been writing for some time, one of the boys raised his hand and said, "But please, sir, we can't do *just seven*, can we?" Of course, there are ten thousand wonders in God.

One of the most fascinating books published in the last thirty years is *Child of Wonder*, Sir John Hammerton's biography of the late Arthur Mee. The book tells how one afternoon Mee crossed Green Park. The sky was pink and gold. The trees were russet. Buckingham Palace and Whitehall were bathed in crimson light, and streaks of fire touched the ripples on the pond. And Arthur Mee paused on the little bridge there, looked about him, and said, "All this is mine." It was true. The world was his – bird and beast, tree and flower, the wealth of the ages, the thrilling present, the lives of men and women – all peculiarly and especially his. And you? Are you intensely alive and intensely aware, so that the earth and its fullness is yours?

That great Scot, Robert Louis Stevenson, had much sickness and ill health in his life. One morning, when he was racked with pain, his wife commented, "I expect you will say this is a glorious day." Between bouts of coughing, the author nodded, and replied, "It is." Looking at the lovely sunshine streaming through the window, then seeing her astonishment, he added, "I refuse to let a row of medicine bottles be the circumference of my horizon." He remembered the psalmist's words: "Look up unto the hills from whence cometh your help, for your help cometh from the Lord." He never lost sight of the wonder of the goodness of God.

Wonder is back in Britain! Thousands of hard hearts are being melted by the Holy Spirit. We are seeing wonderful things: pain-riddled, sick bodies are finding wholeness and healing; a whole generation is turning away from its materialistic gods to praise the Living God; depressed, defeated, despairing, bruised people are being remade, rehabilitated, reborn and revitalized by the peerless, precious Saviour of our souls; empty, purposeless, wasted, twisted lives are finding fulfilment, preciousness, peace and perfection in Jesus. Some of his church has rediscovered the wonder of God!

9

REVIVAL BRINGS LIGHT

"Now I see it; I understand it. I never saw it like that. Is that what it means?" How often in recent times have I heard such things said by old and young, religious and unchurched people. *The Light has come to them.* The Scripture tells us, "Them that have sat in darkness have seen a great light", and "The people in darkness, that dwell in the land of the shadow of death, upon them hath the Light shone." God has said, "Ye were darkness, but *now are ye light.*"

With great endeavour, determination, sacrifice, weariness and fatigue, Christian men and women are bringing the light of life to our generation. They are penetrating the kingdom of darkness with the Kingdom of Light.

The doubters and the pessimists – of which there are many – cannot see any hope; they are not bathed in the light of God, the revival has not touched them. But the children of light are optimistic, hopeful, believing and zealous.

A clergyman working in a city told how he came across a boy standing on the pavement, a broken piece of mirror in his hand, trying to catch the sunlight. He told the minister that on the top floor of the tenement opposite, his sick little sister lay quite helpless. "The sun never shines in her room, and so I thought I would try to send her a little sunshine to cheer her up," said the wee chap. The idea worked, as the clergyman found on going upstairs – the girl was delighted to watch the sun's reflection on the ceiling. We too have it in our power to send light into sunless lives. Victor Hugo once declared, "To shed joy around, to radiate happiness, to cast light upon dark days, is not this to render a service?"

THE GOSPEL OF LIGHT

A friend of mine visited a miniature village some years ago. You could walk down the streets, enjoy the tiny village green, stand outside the baker's, the grocer's, and the paper shop, all these coming up to about the height of the tops of his legs. Then he noticed a crowd of folk standing around a church at the bottom of the village. They were all crowding eagerly round the small spire. When he reached the spot he could see light shining out of the church's windows. It was getting dark, so the effect was all the more impressive. The music of an old-fashioned hymn sounded out from a tiny organ. I like to think of that as a picture of what is happening in the revival. The Gospel of light is drawing great crowds today. Jesus, the Light of the World, is at work in the British Isles. *He is shining through ordinary people.*

A little boy did not know what a saint was. One day he was standing with his father in an old church, looking at a stained-glass window with a picture of a saint in it. As the light shone through the glass, he commented, "Dad, I know what a saint is now. It's someone whom the light shines through."

In this revival Jesus is shining through bakers, postmen, insurance men, builders, refuse collectors, bricklayers, clerks, nurses, soldiers, doctors, gas meter readers and many other people.

Elisabeth Kubler-Ross, in her book *To Live and to Die*, says people are like stained-glass windows: they sparkle and shine when the sun is out, but when the darkness sets in, their true beauty is only revealed if there is light from within. Paul said, "God makes his light shine in our hearts to give us the light of the knowledge of the glory of God" (2 Corinthians 4:6). Let us leave light behind us wherever we go.

One evening, the great preacher Spurgeon, talking to an associate, pointed out the old lamplighter walking along the dark street, using his long pole to set each lamp going. Soon he had disappeared over the hill. Spurgeon commented, "That is how I want to spend my life: lighting lamps in the dark, leaving much light behind me when I finally go over the hill." Is that your ambition? Is that your desire?

THE LIGHT OF THE WORLD

Christianity is a religion of life and light. Jesus said, "I am the light of the world. Whoever follows me will never walk in darkness" (John 8:12). Paul uged the Christians at Philippi to shine as "lights" (AV) "in a crooked and depraved generation" (Philippians 2:15). It is a pity the NIV translates "lights" as "stars", for commentators agree that Paul had in mind the lighthouse on the Isle of Pharos, which was 350 feet high and able to be seen for 100 miles. It was one of the seven wonders of the ancient world. As followers of Christ, we are to be "the light of the world". Matches, candles or even stars do not give out sufficient light. Lighthouses, yes!

The Northumberland lighthouse at Longstone has become automatic. Never again will the lighthouse keeper have to mount the circular stairway of Grace Darling's father's lighthouse to light the lamp. Modern technology and computerization now allow the lighthouse to send out its warning rays automatically in darkness, tempest and fog. So shining for Jesus should be automatic for us Christians. Shining brightly should be second nature to us.

Paul gives two directions for shining brightly: shun darkness and shrug off death. Shunning darkness he defines as "having nothing to do with the fruitless deeds of darkness" (Ephesians 5:11). Shrugging off death he illustrates from a Christian hymn: "Wake up, O sleeper, rise from the dead, and Christ will shine on you" (Ephesians 5:14).

Darkness produces death in the believer's life and witness, so we must shrug it off, just like shrugging off sleepiness when the alarm bell heralds a new day and arouses us from sleep. As we shrug off sleep, ready for breakfast and then for our day's work, so we must shrug off spiritual lethargy and death and let the light of Christ himself be reflected by us. Darkness and death should have no place in the believer's life. We should be shining brightly all the time and in every place.

The old children's hymn was right to say, "Jesus bids us shine with a pure, clear light", though it was wrong to continue, "Like a little candle shining in the night." We are to be like the lighthouse, shedding its warning beams over a wide expanse of sea. God's purpose in our lives is to make us like Jesus. *We are to be a city set on a hill, full of light*, not a candle in a dungeon, hidden from view.

I remember doing a survey of a town in which I was leading a crusade. We first spent an hour or two with the minister, asking how he saw the town, the church and the relationship between the two. I

then asked him for a map of the district, and he
gave me one, with some apologies, because he had
used it as a wall map, with pins in to indicate where
his members lived. I happened to be facing a
window, and as I opened the map I saw the town
with 330 little pinpoints of light shining through all
over the area. To me that was a powerful picture
of what God wants every church to be like.

The world is looking for people who will bring
light into their darkness. God's people in revival are
bringing the Light of Life to their neighbourhood,
their friends and their workmates, because we are
a "light to lighten the Gentiles".

10

THE FAITHFUL FEW

Again and again in the present revival remarkable moves of God's Spirit have occurred in response to the faithfulness of a few dedicated believers.

Two elderly ladies arrived at the Gospel Hall in Blackpool, having only moved into the town some ten days before. The place was cold and empty, although the door had been left open. They stood around for ten minutes. One other person arrived, who whispered a quiet, cool "Good morning" and sat in her usual place near the front of the church, which had been set out with twelve chairs. Then the elderly pastor arrived. He asked why they had come. "For the service," was the reply. He said, "Well, we are closing down here. The church goes up for sale next week." There was a possibility that it might even be turned into a mosque!

Then one of the two old ladies began to weep, saying, "Closing down? You can't do that!" The downcast old pastor was speechless. He looked as if he couldn't believe what she was saying. "You want it to remain open?" he asked. She nodded, still crying. "Will you commit yourself to the work?" the pastor asked. Again she nodded. "Well, if that's the case, perhaps we won't sell – or at least we'll put it off for a few weeks and see what happens."

The outcome was that I went to that church to lead a crusade. A young pastor was found, amidst great sacrifices and prayer, and not least through the vision, persistence and love of the two old ladies. That church now thrives and is part of the evangelical witness in that area of Lancashire.

God's guidance in recent days has become remarkable, as we hear of similar stories of whole new communities or believers being raised up after years of death, waste and emptiness. We see dormant churches coming alive through God's guidance, and through persistent souls like the two ladies in Blackpool waiting and following hard on God's heels.

TROUBLE WITH THE POLICE!

I have seen more miracles in the past few months than in the previous two years – they are proliferating at such a rate! This has got me into trouble with the police. Some of the revival meetings have been so tightly packed that the police have come along with very worried looks on their faces. "You are breaking the law, Rev. Banks – the doors and exits are blocked. You're cramming too many people into the hall." This is the result of Gospel awakening and taking the living, miraculous Lord to the people.

Don't keep Jesus to yourself. The more you give him away, the more you will have of him. Those reaching out together for God to others are experiencing the new wave of revival. We are beginning to march across this nation in God's strength and power. Churches are growing from tiny ecclesiastical groups into living, vibrant, crowded fellowships. Tragic, lonely, tortured souls and minds are coming alive; people bound by strong fetters of lust and sin are flocking to the revival meetings, searching for an experience of God.

A verger was once conducting a party of tourists round a famous and busy abbey, when a member of the group knelt down and prayed. The verger asked him to get up. "But can't I have a few moments of private devotion?" asked the man. "No, we can't 'ave that, or we should soon 'ave people prayin' all over the place!" Churches that have become mere museums are no answer to the spiritual longings of the hungry society around us. Instead God is raising up praying people, not only in churches, but in factories, schools, workshops, homes, universities, council chambers, courts of law and markets; everywhere people are "praying all over the place"!

A DEDICATED MINORITY

The revival meetings are crowded, but God does not necessarily need large numbers to work revival, or to change the world, or to launch his invasion against the devil. God does not look at the outward circumstances; he sees hungry, empty hearts, desperate minds, open vessels. He starts with a faithful few, then a human tide flocks, drawn like a magnet by a people who can pray and who know their God.

A dedicated minority who live by faith in the Son of God are turning this nation around. They are sold out to God, red-hot, Holy Ghost motivated, earnest in intercession. These people are using what talent they have, and are forming the nucleus of revival, the foundation of tomorrow's living, triumphant, loving church, and as a result they are getting into trouble with the law, as Paul and the apostles did in the beginning.

The revival is founded not upon outstanding personalities but upon humble nobodies, obscure people who, when they die, will very soon be forgotten, except by a few who will cherish their memories. But all these people, although unimportant and little known, are living useful, beautiful lives. They are the salt of the earth. Their lives are shining out, piercing the utter darkness of their towns or cities.

Today God is raising up many "little" but big-hearted, powerful, precious, spiritual, godly characters who are beginning to change a whole generation. The whole of creation is on tip-toe to see the wonderful sight of the sons of God coming into their true characters. What a magnificent future God has in store for those who are the "righteousness of God in him"! These people are rescuing the world from tyranny and decay, bringing it into joy, light and marvellous liberty.

SMALL BEGINNINGS

Film director David Putnam, when glancing through a book in a library, caught a few words about Olympic runner Eric Liddel, who forfeited a gold meal in the 1923 Olympics because he would not run in the event, due to the fact that it was staged on a Sunday. Putnam's eye for a good story made him a million pounds through the Oscar-winning film *Chariots of Fire*. One sentence in a book took the Gospel to millions. God often uses the insignificant to achieve his purposes.

The fear of God swept the nation when the Welsh revival broke out. How did it all begin? Through a young man holding his customary prayer meeting in the back hall of his Welsh chapel at Gorseinon! One individual, one moment, one hour, one touch from God can sweep a nation; a whole generation can meet with God. The Lord sometimes uses the trivial and the down-to-earth in powerful ways.

Look at Joseph having a dream (we all dream!) as he lies on his bed. God visits him, and it ends with him sitting on the throne with the king of the most powerful nation of the world at that time. Look at Elijah coming out of the mountains of Gilead – soon he is calling fire down from heaven on the priest of Baal at Carmel, and saves Israel. Look at Amos, a mere fig-picker from Tekoah, finishing as a preacher in royal palaces. Look at the swearing, cursing, bad-mannered fisherman Peter, who goes on to become an apostle. God alone sees both the end and the beginning; he has foreknowledge, all wisdom and insight; nothing is hidden from his eyes.

God is taking obscure people and seemingly insignificant events and using them in amazing ways. He reigns, he is in charge, he is moving! Soon the whole world will be touched from the UK. God is using the "weak things of the world to confound the mighty".

All over this country, almost every day I am on the road preaching. I regularly hear people say, "I saw miracles in a healing service some years ago, and it caused me to believe on the living God, and now I am a keen church worker," or "I was healed of Parkinson's disease in your crusade five years ago, and now I preach all over my county," or "I was only aged four when I was converted in a mission, and now I am a Christian solicitor in Manchester." Here are some other testimonies I have heard: "I was paralysed with multiple sclerosis six years ago, but now I am fit and can do everything, and have started a church; I am pioneering with my husband, who was once an atheist"; "My marriage was breaking up, but God's Word came into the situation, and we are now reconciled and happily married and serving the Lord"; "I was saved after hearing the Gospel, and I am now a full-time pastor in the north of England with a growing, thriving church". *God is using the ordinary to do the extra-ordinary!*

I was crusading in a country town in the East Midlands about twenty years ago. Among those helping me to counsel was a lady in her sixties. She told me she had had a certain young woman in her Bible class back before the War. This person was very strong-willed, deeply interested in what her teacher told her, and an avid reader of the Bible. The lady saw some potential in this youngster and felt that one day she might minister the Word of God. She had such ambition, drive and determination! The lady told the youngster, "I believe that one day you will carry the Bible to the whole of England." She was disappointed when it did not turn out that way. The young woman went off to university and afterwards went into politics. She entered Parliament, then the Government, then the Cabinet, and finally spent a long period in No. 10

Downing Street! The old lady's "prophecy" was fulfilled about seven years ago, when the new Education Act stipulated that there must be Christian religious education in schools and that the morning assemblies must be Christian-based. Thus the school doors were wide open to the Bible as never before. The youth of today have a new opportunity to know God's Word. The old lady was right – this girl she had shaped in her Sunday School class had taken the Bible to the whole nation! That old lady, who died some years ago, is helping us to reach the nation's youth today with the Word of God, because of her influence on that one life so long ago. One ordinary person dedicated to Christ and used by the Holy Spirit can change history.

ORDINARY PEOPLE

Do not underestimate God. The potential of your life in his hands is enormous. Say, "I want to do the best I can for God." God loves to use ordinary people like you. This is what he is doing all over the British Isles today. Abraham Lincoln said, "God must love ordinary people, because he makes so many of them." Indeed he does, and he loves to show his glory through us. What will you do with your life? What will you become? Don't hide in your weakness, ordinariness and failings. See what God does for those who will be revived! Throw yourself at the Saviour's feet; he will lift you, change you, use you.

God used Elijah the ploughman. God called John the Baptist, a simple man of the desert; he filled him with the Holy Spirit and made the whole nation come out and sit at his feet.

Edward E. Hale wrote, "I am only one. But still I am one. I cannot do everything, but I still can do something; and because I cannot do everything I will not refuse to do the something that I can do."

God uses everyone who is dedicated to him, walking in his Spirit; he uses normal, flimsy, simple people. Tough men cowered at the sight of the demonic, fierce Goliath, who was full of brawn, bravado and physical strength. Strong men were powerless against such an enemy. Then came little David with his ten cheese sandwiches for his fighting brothers. Abner had never heard of this young lad David. The King asked, "Who is he?" David was the unknown son of an unknown family, yet he carried Goliath's head home for the dogs to eat, and Israel was victorious. He became the greatest hymn-writer in history – we sing his psalms and songs in our revival meetings all over the UK today. He was just one ordinary young fellow whose condition of heart before God was good and right.

In God's moving today I have met company executives, show-business personalities, ex-criminals, politicians, refuse collectors, builders, barbers, nuclear power station workers, farmers, British Telecom staff, postmen, insurance salesmen, labourers, surgeons, garage mechanics, librarians, nurses, secretaries and even tax collectors! *God is touching and using people in every walk of life*. These are people who love Jesus, whose lives are at his disposal.

Look at Aquilla and Priscilla, the two weavers and tent-makers who opened up their simple home to Paul, Apollos and Timothy. Paul writes of them often – why? – because of the condition of their hearts before the Lord. If your life is surrendered to him, God will use you. In the revival God is raising up thousands of people who are becoming mighty instruments in his hands. He is producing men and women who are made not *by* our times, but by his Spirit *for* our times.

11

REVIVAL PEOPLE

In the present revival I am constantly meeting Christians who have got their priorities right. For example, there is the revived believer who foregoes overtime in this inflationary, money-grabbing, tight-fisted age in order to attend Bible studies. There is the older believer who is badly in need of a rest, but who is so excited about Jesus that he cancels his holiday and spends two weeks on an evangelistic team, working hard to win the indifferent and apa-thetic. There is the elderly lady who makes painful financial sacrifices in order to support missionaries in pagan lands where they have never had a Gospel healing crusade. Such people have the Spirit of Christ in their characters. They, and the many others like them whom I have known, speak vol-umes about the nature of the revival that has come amongst us at this time. The revival is simply *what is in us!*

The Christian character is to be something dis-tinct from that which is admired by the world; it is high above the world's sordid, earthly, pathetic, futile, mundane, materialist and hedonist level. In his or her attitude to money, lifestyle, aims, ambitions and relationships the Christian at odds with the non-Christian world. *It is the life of the Kingdom within us which makes us different.* As Charles Finney put it, "Revival is our beginning to obey God." Do you want a truly Christian pattern to your life? Do you want to live like Jesus showed us? Someone once said that "A Christian is someone who, in spite of this world's cynicism, makes it easy for others to believe in God." We who have received Jesus as Lord and Saviour have the very Spirit of God living right inside us *now*. So with Jesus' help, as we surrender step by step, we can manifest his character in our lives. A person who allows Christ full reign in his or her life becomes a living sermon.

Niebuhr said, "You may be able to compel people to maintain certain minimum standards . . . but the highest spiritual achievements depend not on a push, but a pull." People must be attracted or charmed into righteousness. That loving, winsome, sweet, dedicated, pure life is touching thousands today. The carnal, bustling, shallow, skin-deep, apprehensive, worldly-minded Christian is gradually disappearing into the shadows, and God's men and women are taking the centre of the stage.

I like the story of the old lady who one summer's day walked down a street picking something up from the ground and hiding it in her apron. A policeman watched and became suspicious. He asked what she was doing, but the old lady replied, "That's my business." The policeman became insistent, and when the apron was opened it was full of pieces of broken glass. "Children play barefoot on these hot days, and I was afraid they would cut their feet," was her explanation. Blessed indeed are those who know that the good of other people is their business. This spirit is so strange to our society.

I heard of a man who had a tiff with his local church and pulled his family out of it. For seven years he stayed away, growing bitter as gall. One morning he woke up and told his wife that he was going to ring an elder of the church to tell him that he was coming back. She held her breath as he did so. The family piled into their car and drove to the morning service. Before they could get to the door a most moving thing happened. The entire congregation was waiting and rushed to them, hugging and welcoming them back to their church again. I'm told the congregation worshipped God that morning as never before. Was it any wonder? They had made it easy for even a fallen Christian to be restored.

The revived churches in this nation are manifesting Christ's character – that is the secret of their growth.

A GOOD INFLUENCE

I hear it more and more today as I travel extensively through the British Isles. "I came to this meeting because of the change I saw in my neighbour" or "I found Christ through the honesty of a workmate". whereas years ago many said, "If they are Christians I don't want to know anything about it." There is today an increase of *good Christian living*. Jesus said, "let your light shine before men, that they may see your good deeds and praise your Father in heaven" (Matthew 5:16).

A man was having a little chat with his young son. He was trying to tell him what a Christian should be like and how he should act. When he had finished talking, his son looked at him and asked a stunning question. "Daddy," the boy said, "have I ever met a Christian?" What a telling commentary on the life of that father!

Augustine Birrell once stayed in a fishing village in Cornwall. He was impressed by the atmosphere of sheer goodness in the place. In conversation with an old fisherman, he asked why there was such an atmosphere. The old man replied, "There came a man amongst us, his name was John Wesley." The good influence of Wesley's life and character had remained in the place longs after his death. Similarly, today the Spirit-filled characters of some Christians are influencing many other people for good.

The people we remember with grateful hearts are the people who had values, trust, justice, cleanness, joy, down-to-earth spirituality and kindness. The value of a life lies in the way in which it is spent, not in the way in which it is hoarded. The people whom the world remembers with gratitude are the people who poured out life with a prodigal hand, not the careful souls who jealously hoarded it.

When a young man left home for college, his mother was concerned that he wouldn't keep his room in order. So when she visited him she was not surprised to find his room in total disarray. Papers and books were scattered all over the place. But what shocked her the most were the obscene pictures hanging on the walls.

On his birthday she sent her son a box of presents, including a portrait of Jesus. He thanked her for the gifts, but didn't say anything about the picture. In the spring, when she visited the college again, her son was eager for her to come to his room. On entering she found on the best wall-space the picture of Christ. All the other pictures were gone. Wisely she said, "There is something different about your room. Did you get a new rug?"

"No."

"Is this new paper on the wall?"

"No."

"When I was here before, you had more pictures than now."

"Yes I did, mother, but those other pictures all seemed out of place after that one of Jesus came into the room."

 The presence of Jesus brings conviction, order, purity, wholeness, a new spirit and a new start to people's lives.

DEEP LOVE

Once sinners laughed mockingly at the quarrelling, divided, bigoted Christians; they said sarcastically, "See how they love each other!" But today a new love is growing among some of God's people. I see believers giving time, money, friendship, material goods, care, concern and great compassion to one another. I know many cases where born-again folk have given their holidays away, so that someone more needy than themselves could have one.

Above all, we need to love each other deeply. Sound doctrine without love is barren. Our Lord was full of grace and truth. Both are vital. When I receive bitter letters or shouted protests from people who think they are very "true" Christians, I ask myself, "Where is their love?" Some local churches are destroyed by bitterness and hate. That disgraces Christ and robs the Gospel of its credibility to outsiders.

Love overcomes evil; love can bind us together; love makes us look for the good in one another, not for what we can criticize about each other. Love embraces the outsider with open arms; love crosses barriers of age, race, sex and culture. When Jesus told us to love one another, it was not just so that we could enjoy blessed fellowship. The mutual love of Christians is meant to be an incontrovertible witness to the world – for love, overriding all human differences, can only be of the Spirit.

If we disagree with other Christians, let us meet in love; if we think someone is acting wrongly, we are to go to them in private, not publicly to condemn them. If we see a brother or sister in need we are to come alongside them – we are to care for the sick, those in prison, those suffering the shock of redundancy. Like our Lord, we must have a God-like love for humanity.

It is not religious ceremony that touches folk's hearts in this old, dying world. It is not correctness of church government or soundness of doctrine that kindles the fire. It is the first love of Christ's people for Christ. Let us return to our first love of the Saviour. Ask yourself, "Am I filled with the love of God?" There is nothing like faithful, undying love for one another, for God and for our tortured, sad, loveless world.

FRIENDSHIP AND FELLOWSHIP

A prominent feature of the revival churches is the warm, genuine Christian fellowship and friendship which is found in them.

People anchored in Jesus' love are not going to hurt each other. A person who has allowed Christ full reign in his life becomes a "living sermon", and such people know nothing of isolated Christianity. We are not an "island unto ourselves", as the poet ably said. We love our brothers. Such fellowships grip new people coming in because of their real concern and interest in others. Such Christians are making it easy for others to believe in their God. The churches are made up of all sorts of people: the weak, the strong, the new, the older believers. In such new churches or older revived churches, people are more important than plans or structures. There are the timid, the bold, the inexperienced, the mature, the teens and the elderly all mixing together in love and fellowship and real friendship. As Walter Hearn put it, "There are lots of different kinds of nuts in the Lord's fruitcake"!

I've heard of this friendship breaking out in all sorts of practical ways. Groups of young people on Saturday mornings are clearing the gardens of elderly folk. People who are ill or bereaved receive supportive phone calls from others in the church. If someone is in genuine financial need, the body rallies round and helps, and their problem is solved. I've heard of more than one person receiving a car from another brother who had two, when the former had no means of transport to get him to work or church. This is really the New Testament fellowship as practised by Christ and the early believers. "They had all things in common", we are told in Acts; they shared and met each other's needs. The best friendships are built, *not found*.

What a strong team they had in the Antioch church! Barnabas no doubt chaired some lively meetings amongst the leaders. It was a fellowship that transcended the normal human barriers of race, colour, background and social status.

Dynamic worship backed by consistent teaching, aggressive evangelism and loving friendship is out of this world, and God produces *a church which is unstoppable*. This does not mean that we lose our humanity – we may get angry occasionally – but we have learned not to spoil friendships with anger. If you fly into a rage, you make a bad landing!

Jonathan is one of the great Bible examples of a friend. He said to David, "Whatever your soul desires, I will do it for you." The famous British Artillery Regiment based their motto on David and Jonathan's true friendship; it ran: "We are not divided".

Helping a brother or sister to be all they want to be or should be in Christ, is a solemn privilege and duty, and friendship achieves this. We should be thankful for good friends who tell us our weaknesses, help us in our problems and encourage us to have stronger faith in God. Seek such fellowship, such restored, revived churches, and such real friends in Christ.

12

GOD-GIVEN GIFTS

The man-made effort and the one-man show vanishes in revival. Everyone in the body of Christ counts.

During the First World War my great-uncle was an aircraft mechanic. With those old planes, one man piloted, navigated, dropped the bomb, fired the mounted machine gun, and did just about everything else! But the revival church isn't like that. It's like a Jumbo Jet with hundreds of people in it. They are all flying together to reach their destination. They are all important: each of them has a job to do. We must all humble ourselves and seek our God-ordained gift within Christ's body.

Some years ago I had some young people sent to me by the Home Missions Department of the fellowship of churches I am ordained with. I had youngsters sent to me often. Some were very fine, and many of them have now become excellent ministers. One of these young people said to me, "I would like to get a tent and go into full-time evan-

gelistic work." I replied, "Go and wash my car –
it's very dirty." He protested that this was not "his
job". Finally I got him to do it, but only with great
persuasion. A few weeks later I had a sharp letter
from a church leader involved with organizing these
young people. He said the young trainees "must not
wash the minister's little Lada".

 I wrote in reply, "One will never find one's gift
without humility. One cannot be trusted with big
tasks or gifts from God, until we do the small,
modest task. If you will not get weeds out of the
old age pensioner's garden, how will you weed sinners out of the clutches of the evil one! If you are
above washing a dirty car, how can you be fit to
wash sinners clean by the blood of Jesus? You must
start small!"

That young man never came to anything in the
Kingdom of God, and is not in the ministry today.
Gandhi expected all his closest staff, even his wife
and family, to clean out the toilets, as well as
accompany him at his huge rallies. He expected
them, as he himself practised, to do the same tasks
as the least of his followers would do.

There is scripture which tells us, "To one the gift
of healing, to another tongues, to another the word
of wisdom. . ." An airline pilot does not make the
coffee for the passengers; he gets on with the flying.
A school-teacher does not build extensions to his
classroom; he leaves that to the builder. A ship's

captain does not usually need to haul at a rope; it is enough for him to steer. Use your own gift, and do not envy others theirs. Start small, be willing to do the humble job before using the greater gifts. You will discover your gift and talent in humble service.

A JOB TO DO

There was trouble in the workshop. The tools were having a row. Some blamed it on the hammer; he was much too noisy, so he must go. But the hammer blamed it on the saw; he was constantly going backwards and forwards. No, the saw would not be blamed; he accused the plane; the plane's work was much too shallow, always skimming the surface. But the plane was sure there was someone else at fault; it was the screwdriver, because he was constantly going around in circles. The screwdriver said it was the ruler, because he was always measuring others by his own standard. But the ruler complained about the sandpaper, whom he accused of rubbing people up the wrong way. The sandpaper protested loudly and said there could be no doubt that the drill was the culprit, as everybody knew that he was so boring! With that the carpenter arrived, and the tools fell silent as he picked up each one in turn to finish the pulpit he was making. When completed, it was mounted by many a servant of

God who preached the Word, and multitudes were
✱ blessed. We all have a job to do; we are all called
by God. We all have a part to play.

"It's all right for you — you're called to be an
evangelist, but I'm not." I've lost count of the
number of times I have heard those words! The sad
fact is that on many occasions, I feel they have only
been an excuse — a cop-out disguising an unwilling-
ness to become involved in some area of Christian
ministry.

Sonship is a *now* experience: "Dear friends, *now*
we are children of God" (1 John 3:2). It is an incredible fact, but the moment we received the Lord Jesus
Christ as our Saviour, we became sons, with all
the blessings and advantages of such a position,
including operating our gift. It has been said that
we are adopted by God's grace to be *adapted* to
God's use. Our greatest priority should be to seek
God's will and purpose for our lives. We need to
know all he has in store for us, to know what is
our inheritance, to know what are our own gifts
from him.

J. Hudson Taylor, a key missionary pioneer, tells
of a Chinese pastor who on meeting a young convert, asked him if it was true that he had known
the Lord for three months.

He replied, "Yes, it is blessedly true."

The pastor continued, "And how many have you
won for Jesus?"

"Oh," said the new convert, "I am only a learner, and never possessed a complete New Testament until yesterday."

The Chinese pastor said to him, "Do you use candles in your home?"

"Yes."

"Do you expect the candle to shine only after it is half way down?"

"No, as soon as it is lit."

We are teaching our many converts to "shine" straight away. Find your gift, for as we use our gifts we see amazing results.

Are you adding to your faith? The life that is pleasing to God and which will receive the rich welcome is the life that is reaching onward and upward, pursuing the goal of Christlikeness. It requires both trust and effort. God wants us to add to our Christian walk. We are *all* called to a task for Jesus. There is a ministry and a place for every believer in the body of Christ. There is no reason why any Christian should be spiritually unemployed. The Bible makes it very clear that every Christian has a ministry.

MEMBERS OF THE BODY

In Romans 12, the apostle Paul lists all kinds of member gifts in the body. Some receive spiritual gifts, some have a gift of practical service. Some have a ministry of encouragement, some are gifted in leadership. Indeed, every member's gift is vital to the body of Christ. "The eye cannot say to the hand, 'I don't need you', and the head cannot say to the feet, 'I don't need you' " (1 Corinthians 12:2). All are important. The task of the minister is very clearly defined in Ephesians 4:12: it is "to prepare God's people for works of service, so that the body of Christ may be built up".

Paul said, "Each one should be careful how he builds. For no-one can lay any foundation other than the one already laid, which is Jesus Christ. If any man builds on this foundation using gold, silver, costly stones, wood, hay or straw, his work will be shown for what it is, because the Day will bring it to light. It will be revealed with fire, and the fire will test the quality of each man's work. If what he has built survives, he will receive his reward" (1 Corinthians 3:10–14). God rewards those who build firmly on him and his Word and who come into *all his will and gifts*.

Of course, we thank God for those who are gifted above the normal. But gifts without Christlike character are useless. "May the Lord make your love increase and overflow for each other and for everyone else" (1 Thessalonians 3:12). Here is the hallmark of true Christian profession, and it is the only worthy motive for evangelism.

Many parents have had the experience of attending a school concert to see their child perform. Invariably the child's eyes dart around the audience to locate Mum or Dad. Then a huge grin spreads over their face and they settle down, no longer simply a member of the school group, but with the intention of performing to please Mum or Dad, to win their approval. God would say to us, "Live for the approval, the smile, of the One who called you."

WE'RE ALL IMPORTANT

On one occasion when rehearsing his orchestra, Sir Thomas Beecham suddenly threw up his hands and the music stopped. "Where was the piccolo?" he asked. The poor man with the piccolo was taking a little rest; he would not be missed, he thought. After all, the piccolo was so small. However, the master musician missed it, and the perfect blend of the music was spoilt. Whatever our talent, however small our part, we have to give our utmost for God.

Columba, the early missionary to Britain, one day had two monks brought before him. They had been at loggerheads for some time, each claiming to be the better preacher. Columba listened to their story and then commanded them to stretch their right hands upwards towards heaven. They did so, wondering all the while what the holy man had in mind. "Ah," said Columba, "I see that one of you has a longer arm than the other and can reach slightly higher, but neither of you can reach that white cloud in the sky. Now go and pray for each other and for your people, and you will reach higher than the clouds."

It's true, isn't it? We are all different. Some are tall, some shorter. Some of us can sing, or paint, or are clever with our hands, while others have less obvious talents. Maybe you are a good listener or are fun to be with. There is a place for all of us, and if we work together instead of in rivalry, there's no saying what wonders we can do.

The secret of discovering your gift is, when you have the slightest inclination or feeling in that direction, to move out and do it (after, of course, getting some sound spiritual advice from mature Christian leaders). Smith Wigglesworth used to say, "Don't always wait for special feelings; start in the flesh, and you can finish in the Spirit."

A wise old believer once said, "God supplies the nuts, but the squirrels have to do the cracking." *So get cracking!*

13

Opposition to the Revival

All revivals provoke opposition, and the present one is no exception to the rule.

The people of Israel had many miracles on their journey: the opening of the Red Sea, bread-manna from heaven, fresh water at Mara – but they constantly grumbled! Those who speak against what the Lord is doing today should read Exodus 16:8: "the Lord . . . has heard your grumbling against him". Be careful what you say about God's servants – it may bring chastisement and judgement on you.

Winston Churchill told the story of a young boy who fell into a deep pool in a park. He could not swim, so a man dived in and with great difficulty saved the boy's life. He got the boy out of the pool and took him to his mother. She took the boy in her arms and said to the man, "You left his cap in the pool!" What ingratitude! Instead of a wrong, envious, ungrateful attitude we must have a pure, thankful spirit.

DEAD MEN'S FAITH

Some Christians are critical of the present revival because it isn't identical to the revivals of the past. But, of course, in their own time those old revivals were fresh and new – they too were different to what had happened before. We must not build on dead men's faith; what is past is gone. Don't make a tradition of past revivals, don't stereotype God. God is bringing in power and doing new, exciting things which are different from the things he did in the time of our grandfathers. Of course, many aspects of revival are always the same, such as the exaltation of Christ, conviction, many conversions, great trophies of grace, the humbling of many of the people of God, holiness of life, and many other characteristics which I am sharing in this book. But these things are today happening in a new way. Consequently this revival is being opposed by those who are stereotyped.

Some charismatics come to my meetings and cannot understand why hundreds of folk don't dance, lift their hands or sing Chris Bowater hymns for hours. They cannot see that it is a revival, so they reject it. They forget that many of the people who come to the revival meetings are unsaved. They have nothing to rejoice about – they are in their sins. They can't dance – it's bewildering to them! They are not used to lifting their hands to the Lord, they have hardly ever been to church, they have never heard of the charismatic movement, most don't even know what an evangelist is! But they are being caught up in the revival, as God is touching the unconverted community.

A few years ago in a newspaper article I was accused of being a "racialist preacher". What had I said to provoke such criticism? I had said something at a certain meeting which I had declared hundreds of times before, but on this particular occasion in the city of Gloucester my statement was noted by a newspaper reporter. I had simply told the people at the meeting that Jesus is the only way to God and heaven. One cannot know God through following the Buddha or Mohammed or Krishna or Confucius or the Rev. Moon. Christ is exclusive, he is the only way to be saved; all other ways are false religions. We are witnessing a marked increase in opposition to the revival.

PROPHETS ARE UNPOPULAR

We live in a society that is becoming more and more hostile towards those who live by the standards of God's Kingdom. Even the prophets were sometimes affected by opposition; Jeremiah became so discouraged by it that he wanted to quit preaching. Persecution takes its toll. In this move of God, some Christians have given up under pressure, in spite of the abundant miracles, conversions and precious movings of the Spirit which they have seen. Instead they have gone to "easier churches" where little is happening and where there is no satanic pressure against them. Like Obadiah, who went off looking for grass with Ahab, instead of praying earnestly with Elijah for rain, they want to go to heaven on "flowery beds of ease". Some preachers resign after waiting for the revival for twenty-five years. When it finally comes, it's too much for them.

In revival some of your Christian friends will part company with you. Paul himself experienced this: "Demas has forsaken me", he complained, and John wrote, "Diotrephes has caused me some trouble." But also there arises fresh blood – the Aquillas and Priscillas who open their hearts and homes to God's moving.

The world hates the Micahs who say, "Thus saith the Lord." As G. Campbell Morgan said, "The world hates Christian people, that is, if they see Christ in them." Jesus said, "If you belonged to the world, it would love you as its own. As it is, you do not belong to the world. . . That is why the world hates you" (John 15:19). Prophets (or anyone who lives close to Jesus) are never popular with the Pharisees. One generation stones the evangelists, the next builds statues and sepulchres to them. Joseph Parker declared, "There are those today who would clasp the hands of Bunyan, who would not admit a living Bunyan to fellowship."

I stood on the outskirts of Portsmouth recently, when preaching in the lively, growing Langstone Christian Fellowship. I stood on the spot where John Wesley preached his last open-air sermon. He was stoned, scorned and pulled from his horse in his day; he was written against, and churches closed to him all over Britain. Yet today even a tree beside which he preached is kept as a memorial.

We build edifices to remember those whom our predecessors shunned and rejected. Organized religion is the worst culprit. It hates the preachers it cannot control; it despises the lone dissenter, the preacher whose only headquarters is heaven and whose Superintendent is God. Revival is always prayed for and needed, but never wanted when at last it comes. An apathetic church would rather have the status-quo preachers.

When I was in Gloucester a short time ago, it was the anniversary of the birth of George Whitfield. The same clergymen who packed that anniversary service were silent when I stood for the name of Jesus against Islam. They don't mind a dead prophet, but they did not welcome a living one. Even some charismatic churches would not get involved, but non-renewed Brethren and Baptists ran to my aid.

OPPOSITION — HOW TO COPE WITH IT

Today young people, converted wives with unsaved husbands, men with hardened wives, grandparents with awkward grandchildren, business partners newly born again with worldly associates, men in factories facing those who seek to sack them because they know Jesus, teenagers with aggressively anti-Christian parents — all these people are facing the wrath of the devil. What can we do in the face of such opposition? Here is some advice.

First, don't kick against the goad. Take it on the chin and come back up fighting. As the old boxers' saying goes, "In the ring there is nowhere to hide." Don't take revenge, but do the opposite — *love your persecutors*. Believers must not behave as the world does. We should turn the cheek, as Jesus said. Seeking to hit back only weakens our hand. We are to encourage, comfort, help and take care of each other in the faith, especially those under attack, for it is the way of Christ.

Secondly, face the persecution. Go through it with God, have no self-pity, resign yourself to it. In Joseph Conrad's bestseller *Typhoon*, a seaman on a ship faces a terrific storm. Tossed to and fro, almost capsized, he tells the captain, "Always face it, Captain Macquire, that's the way to get through the storm." Or, in the words of the old boxing term, "Roll with the punch." Paul urged us to let impossible situations and trials shape us for good.

Finally, learn from your experience of persecution. We must learn from life's trials and turn them to good. Paul and Peter both knew about this from their own experience: "These [trials] have come so that your faith – of greater worth than gold . . . may be proved genuine and may result in praise, glory and honour" (1 Peter 1:7); "Out of the most severe trial, their overflowing joy . . . welled up" (2 Corinthains 8:2). We can use the burdens and heartaches of opposition to take us higher in Christ.

The more I study the careers of people of achievement, the more convinced I am that a surprisingly large number succeeded because they started out with handicaps that spurred them on to great endeavour and great rewards. As William James said, "Our infirmities help us unexpectedly." Helen Keller's brilliant career was inspired and made possible by her blindness and deafness. If Tchaikovsky had not been frustrated and driven almost to suicide by his tragic marriage, if his own life had not been pathetic, he probably would never have been able to compose his immortal *Symphonie Pathétique*. If Dostoevsky and Tolstoy had not led tortured lives, they would probably never have been able to write their outstanding novels. Paul said, "suffering produces perseverance; perseverance, character; and character, hope" (Romans 5:3–4).

Many people in the revival are facing opposition

and are "coming through shining" for Jesus our Lord.

14

Aspects of the Revival

In this chapter I want to talk about some of the aspects of the revival which is presently sweeping through the nation.

THE JUDGEMENT OF GOD

Judgement is one of the forgotten aspects of revival, but it is very much part and parcel of the present move of God's Spirit.

Scripture contains many stories about God's judgement. There is the very sobering case of Ananias and Sapphira in the Book of Acts. Because of their deceit they were a hindrance to revival, and so God forcibly removed them from the church. Many years ago Dr Alex Whyte, preaching to a packed, fashionable evangelical congregation in Edinburgh, said, "You are all praying for revival, but if God answered, there would be a stream of ambulances outside taking you to the mortuary!" The God who answers by fire answers by judgement too!

In Britain today we are seeing God's judgement. A young pastor came from a Bible college and took over a troublesome little church on the east coast. One pastor after another had worked there; none had stayed there long, because there was continuous bickering and squabbling. The new man had only been there a week or two, and went to visit one of the main troublemakers for many years. When he went to the door, the man refused to let the pastor in, and shouted at him and waved his fist. Going red in the face, he argued with the pastor, who innocently lifted his hand, pointing to the heavens, and said, "Brother, the Lord. . ." He could not get any more words out, as the *man dropped dead on the spot*. To the pastor's amazement, it soon got around in the little town that he had extraordinary power! He only had to say, "In the name of the Lord" and anything could happen. Soon the whole church became silent, love broke out, old enemies became friends, new people flooded in, and the fear of God came on the town and the church. From a small, troublesome church, it became peaceful, eveangelistic and prayerful, and grew and grew until an extension had to be built on. Later it set up a daughter church in that town. The fear of God is coming again.

I stood in the large Victorian mission hall in the West End of London, hundreds waited for healing and laying on of hands and prayers. As we moved along inch by inch, God was touching and healing many folk.

Then suddenly I stopped and eyed a man behind the person I was to pray for next. A strange feeling came over me; I had never felt like it before, and I have never felt like it since. *"Don't pray for him, he's not real,"* came a clear, quiet, inner witness. I am not given to great revelations very often, and had never had such clear direction or such a thought before. I have always had a great love for the sick, and I always want to pray for everyone. But the message was clear: I must not pray for that man.

As he stood before me, strangely the whole congregation fell silent, so I could not speak quietly to him or slip him out the side door to explain. I said aloud, "I cannot pray for you; I don't believe you have a real sickness." Then amazingly, I said, "You are planted here. You are acting deceitfully." I bit my lip – why on earth did I say that? What if it was my imagination? He looked stunned; the whole congregation gasped. My own team had never heard me say such a thing; it was quite out of character.

Then a man rushed up with a camera, and tried to take a snap. Then we learned the truth. Some corrupt pressmen had planned it all. They had said, "Let's see if this man really is in touch with God. Let's fool him and show him up." This was their idea, but it didn't turn out the way they had planned. They literally ran out of the building. I believe it was a case of God's judgement at work.

There are some who discover too late that they have taken the wrong turning in life. Cardinal Wolsey was Henry VIII's great Prime Minister. For a time he flourished; and then the policy of the king demanded that Wolsey be jettisoned. For a time Wolsey managed to buy security, but in the end his execution came. As he lay awaiting the end, he talked to the Lieutenant of the Tower. "Master Knygton," he said, "had I but served God as diligently as I have served the king, he would not have given me over in my grey hairs. But this is my due reward for my pains and study, not regarding my service to God, but only my duty to my prince." Wolsey had made a mistake. He had not realized where he was going. The end was tragedy.

God's judgement is manifested not only for the benefit of his church but also for the whole lost world. Man must be shown the power of God. Herod acted like a wild animal after opposing the will of God; severe punishment came to Bar-Jesus on the isle of Cyprus, when he sought to oppose Paul and Barnabas in the Gospel work; Simon, who tried to manufacture the gifts of God after the Jerusalem revival, was soon bound by the Spirit of God; those who touched the Ark of the Covenant in the Old Testament were struck dead on the spot. The awe and fear of God sweeps in and touches a whole nation at such times.

Today the churches which shun the revival will be judged by God. Revival always includes an element of judgement, and it is discernible already.

THE UNPREDICTABLE GOD

One of the refreshing joys of the revival is the surprise which God pulls on us so often. Someone once said that every encounter with God has within it the glory of surprise. Certainly, in Scripture God is always turning the tables in unusual ways. For instance, think of Gideon. God cut his army down to a hopeless 300 men "armed" with jars and flaming torches, yet they were victorious against the Midianites. Look at Moses and his staff, working miracle after miracle; or prophecy coming through Baalam's ass. Boris Pasternak said, "Surprise is the greatest gift that life can grant us."

Very often God's people want to plan how God should do it. They want it all prim and proper, and nothing out of the ordinary, all signed and sealed; they want to control God. The disciples were incredulous when the three women told them that Christ was risen (Luke 24:11). Thomas could not believe the Lord had spoken to his friends unless he was given personal evidence (John 20:25).

Recently I was at a packed revival meeting in central Birmingham. Many people had been blessed and released, seeing, hearing, walking again. As I

moved through the crowd I suddenly felt led to
touch the head of a certain woman. She had given
no indication of being sick. I did not know her —
why did I touch that one woman in the middle of
a packed crowd? She cried out as I walked past.
Someone came running to me afterwards to tell me
what had happened. Her hand had been paralysed
for eighteen months; she was in agony, with all the
tendons pulled out. Her hand had suddenly fallen
back into place, the pain had vanished, she could
use it fully, *all in seconds*. He is an astonishing God!

I had run out of money on a missionary journey.
I had virtually nothing left, and yet I had many
expenses and much travel ahead in a poor country,
where multitudes waited to hear of Christ. But God
miraculously sent money into my locked case! When
I went to my case to count my money once more, I
found that I now had enough for all my needs! He
is a miraculous, surprising God.

In the present revival God is constantly doing the
unexpected. Sinners are being forgiven, worn-out
lives are being rejuvenated, dreams are being made
real, hopes are being fulfilled, the chronically sick
are being cured, broken homes are being reunited
with peace and joy. However uncertain the future
may be, there is a constantly accessible source of
hope. In every day of darkness there is the promise
of God's inextinguishable light; in every crisis or
tragedy, the resources to overcome are available.

C. Fields, a leader in the United Reformed Church, wrote: "The constantly unpredictable God has given himself to us through Jesus Christ." Today and tomorrow the glorious God will give himself to a degree beyond all that can be imagined. If you are willing and prepared to be surprised, you will be, and every surprise will be sheer delight.

A young convert in this present move of the Spirit was out for a walk in the country, when on a lonely footpath an old man passed by. He was bent over, struggling, clearly with a painful back, moving slowly by. The young man suddenly stopped and said, "Jesus Christ can heal your back!" The old man looked at him, startled, thinking he had met a maniac. The young man laid hands on him and said, "I am going to pray for you," which he did, and then walked off. About ten months later an elderly man came up to him at work. The man was doing odd jobs around the warehouse, part time. "Do you remember me?" he asked the young Christian. It was the old man he had prayed for! He was now following Christ, attending a local church regularly.

In London about forty years ago, a large, highly organized evangelistic mission was planned, led by a very well-known American preacher. Thousands of Christians were mobilized, large finances were expended, and much hard work was done. The result was a good mission – but there was no revival. At the same time, two old women were praying in the north of Scotland. They had no church support or organization, and their preacher was not well known, but the result was a remarkable revival. Nothing has been seen like it since, until this present move of the Lord today.

On some occasions I have been invited to preach at posh, large evangelical churches. There were big congregations, many stewards, excellent control and organization, plenty of counsellors and workers, marvellous music and worship, *but no breakthrough*. The people got excited if there were a hundred converts and some good healings, but that is not a revival!

But on other occasions I have preached at less impressive churches. It might be a church in a rough part of a big city. The pastor has to do a full-time secular job and does his pastoring in his spare time, so he is exhausted. There is no choir, no sophistication, no mass offerings, no slick organization – and yet *a revival happens*. A fifth of the town turns out, 500 are converted, miracles flow from my fingertips, it is easy to get nearly everyone healed – God is there! It is superior, masterly, alive, free, astonishing, full of unceasing surprises, exciting beyond explanation. The God of wonders and marvels displays his power!

The Lord often surprises us, working powerfully when we least expect it. He is the unpredictable God!

REVIVAL WINS OUR LOVED ONES

One of the precious happenings of these momentous days is the salvation or restoring of many unsaved or backslidden family members. Everywhere I go I hear, "My brother has come to the Lord" or "My sister has just got saved" or "Mum repented and found the Saviour last week".

In this generation many Christians have lost the sense of the grave danger that their unsaved or backslidden family members are in. I shall never forget the text which hung on the wall of my bedroom when I was a boy. The last thing I saw at night and the first thing I saw in the morning was a single large eye on a white card and the words, "Thou, God, seest me." I am ready to agree that much in the faith of our fathers ought to be discarded, but they had an awareness of *what is right and what is wrong*. It is the lack of this which is so largely responsible for the careless living of our day. And, oddly enough, those who are afraid to do wrong are in fact the happiest people. It is those who do as they please and live for themselves who find that a false way of living brings only disillusionment and bitterness. To live knowing that God watches and cares is the truly rewarding way of life.

These have been dark times. As Jay Gould puts it, "Things are not as bad as they seem – they

couldn't be!" But the tide turns at *low water*, and
that is now happening, thank God.

A little girl was playing with her dolls. There was
no light on and the evening had come, and she could
hardly see her dolls. She called out for some light,
saying, "Mummy, let's put the dark out!" We must
rescue our loved ones from the darkness. The Psalmist said, "In thy light we shall see" (Psalm 36:9),
and again, "unto the upright there ariseth light in
the darkness" (112:4).

God knows your family by name. He cares for
every one of them and wants to bring them into his
Kingdom. I like the story of the local Council official
who was making house-to-house calls to find out
how many people were living in a certain district..
When he enquired at one house as to how many
people lived there, the mother of the house began,
"Well, there's Horace, and Jim, and Nelly, and
Mary, and. . ." The official interrupted, "I don't
need names, madam, I just want numbers." "They
haven't got numbers," retorted the woman indig-
nantly, "they've all got names!" God knows all of
us by name.

Remember, you may be the only light your relatives will ever see; they are wandering in the highways and byways of life, somewhere in the darkness.
We are believing in this revival that because we
are now saved, salvation is also available for our
household. "Believe in the Lord Jesus, and you will

be saved – you and your household" (Acts 16:31). We are believing more than ever that God will touch our relatives and bring them into the Kingdom.

Years ago I won my own father to Christ. My wife's uncle came 400 miles to attend one of my meetings. A tough businessman, he had never been interested in our ministry or in going to church or spiritual things. He got saved on the spot and was the first one at the altar that night!

We cannot sit still and just leave our relatives to die and go to hell. There is a new earnestness now for many to win their relatives. We must shine, we must reach out to them.

I know the son of a minister who had seen signs, wonders and miracles all his life, but in his teens he became a real rebel, falling into every type of sinful habit and transgression. He brought great heartache to his devoted Christian family. They hung on for him. Ten years later, at three o'clock in the morning, the son telephoned his father. The worried father put the phone to his ear, and heard the greatest news a dad could get: "I'm so sorry. I've been such a bad son to you. I've really come to the Lord tonight. I'm broken, I fear God, I'm giving him all my life." That news was worth hanging on for! Today that son is preaching the Gospel all over Britain.

Maybe your dear ones have been overcome by evil powers. You think they will never come home, but there is hope! *You are the key*. If you will die to yourself and pour out your heart and life for them, one day – even soon – you will rejoice to see the prodigals coming home to the Father.

In many places today believers are praying for their unsaved relatives and friends. They are pleading for them with new earnestness, praying in the Holy Ghost, using the name of Jesus to drive devils away from them, calling them into the Kingdom with divine authority. Many are writing a letter, making a phone call, paying a visit, taking them out for a meal or to the theatre, making contact.

We don't realize the awful curse they are under. The enemy has got his hands on them. We must bind the devils who are attacking and surrounding many believers' homes. We have power and authority over all devils, the Scripture tells us. For untold legions of demons have been unleashed on our generation. Many relatives of Christians are a shame to the neighbourhood and their parents. Even some children and grandchildren of ministers are sinning and causing much despair. Recently it was found that at least half of the children of the ministers of one denomination were not following the Lord. In one large, popular evangelical church it was discovered that one third of the parents had children who were far away from God.

Is the devil destroying your family? Use the name of Jesus to drive him out! Jesus said: "I have given you authority to trample on snakes and scorpions, and to overcome all the power of the enemy; nothing will harm you" (Luke 10:19). *Your loved ones are going to come to Jesus*. Say it, repeat it every day with that scripture, pray it in Jesus' name . . . until it comes to pass. Don't quit, don't despair, don't give up. Love them, care for them, be firm, give no quarter to sin, fight it in the heavenlies. Pray it through: *they are going to be set free*, free from the power of the evil one, free to serve the Living God for the rest of their lives.

A lady came 300 miles to a service I was holding; her husband reluctantly accompanied her. He had never been interested in spiritual things. She got blessed, but he got saved and healed and has been on fire for God ever since! After thirty-five years of married life and little interest in God, he is now broken, saved and burning for Christ. Don't give up! "He would have destroyed them . . . had not one stood in the breach" (Psalm 106:23).

Pauline had an atheist husband. She was healed of multiple sclerosis, and went home and won her husband to Jesus. He is now a co-pastor in a church.

Jim, another atheist, had a fractured spine. He had never been to church in his life. He was brought along to a revival meeting by his niece. He got converted and was wonderfully, miraculously and instantly healed. He went home and within a few weeks won his wife to Christ. Both now work for God, and he is a deacon in a church.

I have seen some of my long-lost relatives saved in the last five years: four aunts, two uncles, a cousin and her husband and his mother.

Revival means winning lost families. Defeat the devil, call on the miracle-worker, our Lord Jesus Christ, to help you. God wants your relatives!

REVIVAL DEFENDS THE FAITH

When I am interviewed on TV or radio, I am often introduced as "a defender of the faith". I am proud that such a phrase is used of me, although sometimes it is said in a sarcastic manner! At other times the media people call me a "fundamentalist". Although I am certainly fundamental on the Word of God, believing completely in its inerrancy, the word has connotations today with false religions such as Islam and other groups including many fanatics, so I am not so keen on this term.

The real revival amongst us now has sparked off a vigorous defence of the essentials and basics of the faith "handed down to the saints", such as the imputed righteousness of Christ, the blood of Christ, justification by faith, restitution, repentance, substitution, propitiation, the second coming of Christ, healing in the atonement etc.

In ancient Greece the Spartans were always proverbial for their courage. They might lack the finer virtues of the more cultured Athenians, but no one ever questioned their courage and their loyalty. In his life of the Spartan King Lycurgus, Plutarch tells a great story. There was a certain Spartan wrestler competing at the Olympic Games. An attempt was made to buy him off by the offer of a large sum of money. He completely refused it. After a long struggle he outwrestled his opponent and won his victory. He was asked, "What advantage, O Spartan, have you gained from your victory?" He answered with a smile, "I shall stand in front of my king when I fight our enemies." The greatest privilege of which the Spartan could conceive was to defend his king, if need be with his life, in the day of battle.

Our great privilege at the end of this century is to see a revival of the true faith, and a firm defence before the world of the doctrines of Christ. We are finding, however, that the best way to defend the faith is not by negative protests – barking old theology that is now meaningless – but by *knowing the doctrine* in experience, heart and mind; by an outward-looking, anointed, Spirit-filled, joyous, up-to-date, attractive communication; by going out to the whole world. This is the best way to spread the truth of Christ everywhere. The first apostles "filled Jerusalem with the doctrine", Acts tells us. Spurgeon said, "The Bible is always a new book; there is nothing stale in it." Hosea said of the Word of God, "It is a fire in my bones."

In this revival there is a new, bold declaration of the biblical, apostolic faith.

15

POWER THROUGH PURITY

In today's revival confessions of past sinfulness have become more the rule than the rarity. God's people are asking for forgiveness, for cleansing from past sins, prejudices and excesses. As a result they are becoming a pure and humble people.

Sometimes I hear of churches having a "sorting out", with numbers dropping off; then I hear a year later of huge increases. Sometimes a decrease goes before an increase in revival, like Gideon's band being purged, till only the true, watchful ones were left. John Wesley wrote in his journal of a conversation in which he said, "We are having a wonderful revival." He was asked how many were added to the church, and replied, "None, but twenty left."

A revival is a cleaning and purging before an enduing of power. Today, compromise rules in many circles, so there is no power. God wants a people who will stand up and tackle the devils of this world. He wants a daring, courageous, fearful, pure, powerful people. William Booth said, "The measure of your power depends on the measure of your surrender." Arthur Birt used to say, "God is not looking for my ability, he is looking for my availability."

We must put ourselves in the hands of the purifying, scouring, purging, searing, burning, blazing God who will cleanse and empower us. *Dare to let God deal with you.* There is power in purity and surrender. Yield, give yourself away. We can only do the impossible, know his power, win through, capture our generation, feed the down-and-out, deliver the deranged, cure the sick, work miracles and win many new converts from sin and damnation by being melted, made whole and purified ourselves. David said God desires "truth in the inner parts" (Psalm 51:6).

Let him root out the irregular, the incorrect, the impure, the unholy in you; let him change you, give you *his* power, trust you with his gifts. Jesus said, "Be perfect, as your heavenly Father is perfect" (Matthew 5:48).

After Louis XVI, King of France, was beheaded in the French Revolution, his son was placed in the custody of brutal people who tried to make him forget that he was the son of a king and that he had a duty to maintain high standards of conduct. They did their best to corrupt the boy's morals, but because he came from royal parents, he refused to do anything evil. He remained loyal to the teachings he had received about right and wrong. In the face of temptation he was heard to say, "I cannot do that, for I am the son of a king."

God is raising up a people who live by the King's standards and by the light of the Holy Spirit, a people who will not blemish themselves in this world's filth. They are a people who are *purged but powerful.* As the hymn says:

When through fiery trials thy pathway shall lie,
His grace all-sufficient shall be thy supply.
The flame shall not hurt thee, his only design
Thy dross to consume and thy gold to refine.

CHRISTLIKE PEOPLE

One of the features of the revival is that it is producing Christlike people. The New Testament emphasizes that our behaviour is the true evidence of our conversion. Jesus said, "All men will know that you are my disciples if you love one another" (John 13:35). The sign of genuine discipleship is that when people look at us, they see the character of God.

We will not be perfect in this life, for we "are being transformed into his likeness with ever-increasing glory" (2 Corinthians 3:18). Growing in godliness is a continuing process. God is unchanging in his holiness and in his demand for holiness and integrity in our lives. "Holy, holy, holy is the Lord

God Almighty, who was, and is, and is to come"
(Revelation 4:8). A truly holy man is a Christlike
man.

How can we become holy? There is no short cut
here. We have to take in before we can give out.
We cannot afford to neglect the means of grace.
Above all, we must spend much time with our Lord.
The Psalmist wrote, "Those who look to him are
radiant" (Psalm 34:5).

We must not treat sacred things flippantly. At a
time when blasphemy is rife and the sacred is cast
into the gutter, we must be most careful to maintain
holy standards. Holiness unto the Lord must be
written over all we do. There is great freedom in
submitting fully to Christ. This is the key to pleasing
him and becoming like him. God has sworn to make
us holy.

Bonhoeffer wrote, "The follower of Christ is in
the light and gives light, only so long as he looks
simply to Christ and at nothing else in the world."

The greatest of all the Greek kings was Alexander
the Great, the man who before he was thirty wept
because there were no more worlds left to conquer.
The most illuminating story of Alexander comes
from his Persian campaigns. He had put Darius into
a position in which ultimate defeat was certain.
Darius recognized this and offered Alexander terms
which were very favourable. He offered Alexander
a great ransom for the captives which had been

taken, a mutual alliance, and the hand of one of his daughters in marriage. All this Darius offered, if Alexander would halt and stay his hand and be content with what he had already won. Alexander told Parmenio, his chief of staff, about the terms which had been offered. Parmenio said, "If I were you I would accept them." And Alexander replied, "So would I – if I were Parmenio." Alexander was Alexander, and for him nothing less than absolute victory would do. A lesser man would be well content with lesser things, but for Alexander it was all or nothing.

God wants us to be pure in a grossly impure world. He wants us to have clean hands and hearts. He wants us to be a people of character, reliability, faithfulness, integrity and unselfishness; he wants us to be caring, true to our word, clean in mind, pure in motive, honest in conduct. He wants from us a fruitful, mature spiritual life, a heart on fire for him.

Jesus pointed out, "By their fruit you will recognize them. Do people pick grapes from thornbushes, or figs from thistles? Likewise every good tree bears good fruit, but a bad tree bears bad fruit. A good tree cannot bear bad fruit, and a bad tree cannot bear good fruit. Every tree that does not bear good fruit is cut down and thrown into the fire. Thus, by their fruit you will recognize them" (Matthew 7:16).

In revived churches across Britain we are emphasizing that we must keep a watch on our lives, our standards, our behaviour – it must be good, correct and upright. As the word says "The Lord does not look at the things man looks at. Man looks at the outward appearance, but the Lord looks at the heart" (1 Samuel 16:7).

The Gospel of the revival is not only an escape route from hell to heaven, but is also the means whereby the Spirit of God remakes people, so that they display the character and glory of God.

THE INDWELLING CHRIST

Job pointed out that God looks for a pure life, a fine character, an example, an integrity and uprightness from his people: "Does he not see my ways and count my every step?" (Job 31:4). God wants to do a work inside us; he wants to plant his nature, righteousness and goodness in us. Our biggest spiritual struggle is to allow God to do that work, and to yield our will to practice his precepts and turn away from the world's tawdry, false standards. God is unchanging in his holiness and in his demand for integrity and goodness in our lives.

The greatest fact in all of history is that the Lord has chosen to come and dwell in us. Think of it! Almighty God lives in us. The Bible teaches that if you want a fruitful life, if you want to overcome temptation, if you want power and authority, then *Christ himself must do it in you*. That discovery revolutionized my life! "If anyone is in Christ, he is a new creation; the old has gone, the new has come" (2 Corinthians 5:17). No one can live the Christian life except Christ himself. Only as he dwells in us and we submit to his presence can the Christian life be lived as it's meant to be – that is, on the supernatural level. Too many Christians believe that if they pray enough, read enough and work enough, they will be victorious. That is the essence of flesh, the essence of self. It cannot be done. We cannot earn our own victories through any self-effort, anymore than we could earn our own salvation.

Have you discovered the revolutionary impact of the Christ-centred life? We must allow Christ to be himself in us. Galatians 2:20 reads: "It is no longer I who live, but Christ who lives in me." Someone has said that the greatest need today is not only for more Christians, but for people who are more Christian. J. B. Phillips' translation of Colossians 1:10 reads: "We also pray for you that your outward lives [i.e. your goodness] which men see, may bring credit to your master's name."

The Bible does not glamourize its characters; it shows them "warts and all". But it also shows their basic purity, godliness and goodness; they wanted to glorify God above all. Years after Christ left the earth, he was still the power, the goodness and the love in the disciples. At one town they worked a great miracle by Jesus' power. The people flocked to worship them (Acts 3:12–16). The apostles said, "Why do you stare at us, as if by our own godliness we made this man to walk?" It was Jesus who healed him, even though he was no longer with them physically. His Spirit, his character, his goodness, was in them.

A REVIVAL OF INTEGRITY

Lack of integrity, dishonesty, double standards, secret under-the-table dealings, back-scratching, self-promotion, giving friends a leg up – all these have been prominent in the church, and in particular in the ministry, over the years, but now, due to God's moving by his Spirit they are on the wane.

I increasingly meet ministers who refuse to water down the Gospel for the sake of professional advantage. They may well still be the minority, but they are a sizeable one.

It is said of Dr Johnson, the erudite scholar of the eighteenth century, that he was so accustomed to telling the truth that he never gave an ambiguous answer to any question. A lady acquaintance once asked him why he was never invited to dine at the tables of the great, to which Johnson replied, "I do not know any cause, unless it is that lords and ladies do not always like to hear the truth, which, thank God, I am in the habit of speaking." Men of integrity gain only one kind of friend – true ones.

A friend tells me that one evening he overheard two schoolboys deep in conversation at the pavement edge. "All right," said one, "we'll make it nine in the morning, sharp. Promise you'll be there on your honour." The other laughed scornfully. "Don't talk soft," he said. "My dad never says things like that. He justs says he'll do it, and it's as good as done." Can we have too many folk whose word is their bond?

The talk in revival circles is often, "How can I help you, brother?" "Can I pray with you, sister?" "What has God done for you today, friend?" Ask yourself, "Am I scrupulously pure? Is there any secret sin or wicked way with me? Do I love the poor, help the homeless, care for the housebound?"

This is what the spiritual revival is doing: it is raising up a whole new breed of devoted men and women who are true to their word and who desire above all to please God in every area of their lives.

16

REVIVAL THROUGH COMMITMENT

One young man, who is such a gracious witness to Christ, told me how after a college course the two leading lecturers, both agnostics, asked him about the reality of Christ. They had been touched through his consecrated, holy life, by his consistent, honest living and quiet witness amongst them. In the present revival power is being manifested through many people whose lives are characterized by this 100 per cent consecration to Jesus.

An amusing story is told about a man whose home was on the border that separated the North from the South during the American Civil War. He didn't want to take sides, so he wore a Confederate Army jacket and Union Army trousers. But he ran into trouble. The Union soldiers shot at his jacket and the Confederates shot him in the pants! Similarly, you cannot be half-hearted about God and his Kingdom — you must have only one total master.

The people who are finding God's power today are those who have got their priorities right — they belong wholly to Jesus. This was the key to the rapid growth of the early church: "they gave themselves first to the Lord" (2 Corinthians 8:5). That is the secret. They gave themselves first to the Lord, they held nothing back but gave everything – their time, their energy, their money, their talents and their gifts. It is that sort of giving and unrestrained commitment that marks out a revived people, because it is the sort of giving that characterized Jesus.

Can I challenge you to renew your commitment to the Kingdom of God? Remember that before you offered your life to Jesus, he was offering his life to you. There is a priority of grace that is demonstrated in the coming of Christ, in his life and death and glorious resurrection.

IS YOUR LIFE SURRENDERED?

As Jesus explains: "If Satan drives out Satan, he is divided against himself. . . *But if I drive out demons by the Spirit of God, then the kingdom of God has come upon you* . . . how can anyone enter a strong man's house and carry off his possessions unless he first ties up the strong man?" (Matthew 12:26, 28–29). There is only one way for evil to be defeated in our lives, and that is by the overwhelming power of goodness and love. So if our lives are to be possessed by Jesus' love and goodness, then the strong man has to be bound, defeated and destroyed. Jesus wants to take over our lives and establish his rule and reign within us, which is the mark of his Kingdom, but first the strong man of pride, rebellion and self-assertion must be bound. Is your life surrendered? Who is in control? Does Jesus reign?

Jesus often talked about priorities. He did so because even among life's important things, some are more important than others, and as life gets pared down to the irreducible minimum, we ask: What is it that I cannot live without? What are the crucial things in my life? What are my priorities?

Jesus said, "Seek first the Kingdom". That is life's irreducible minimum. Whatever it is that you want from life, be it happiness, fulfilment, success, the blessing of God, then here is the priority for you – seek first the Kingdom.

The Bible is full of examples of people who put other things first. A teacher of the law says to Jesus, "I will follow you wherever you go." Jesus reminds him that foxes have holes, but the Son of Man has nowhere to lay his head. The teacher soon disappears when he realizes the cost of 100 per cent discipleship. The rich young ruler, who is looking for assurance of heaven, is told by Jesus to get rid of his "god", his materialistic spirit – soon he vanishes. Then there is the case of the man who says he must first bury his father. By that he doesn't mean a simple funeral service, but years of tying up legal matters, living out his inheritance, many tasks that others could do. In other words, it was an excuse – "Someday I'll be committed" it meant.

Why did Germany go down to a monster like Hitler in the 1930s? Because church leaders put things other than Jesus first. Hitler said to Herman Rausling, "The pastors will dig their own graves, they will betray their God. . . They will betray anything for the sake of their miserable jobs and income." How true, how sad, and what a disaster for the world! 100 per cent-ers would have stopped that evil man. We need to turn the whole world from the disasters that stalk us today, and turn them to the Cross.

It is not time to be spectators, it is time to be protagonists of God's work as a part of redemptive history. It is time to make him our priority. *Christ must be first, last and all in between*. Let him establish his kingship, his rule, his reign over you. Seek first the Kingdom of God.

It is in such *dying* people that we are seeing resurrection, revival, renewal and real fruitfulness in these heart-moving days.

THE COST OF DISCIPLESHIP

A young woman was looking for a husband. She was very attractive and had many offers, but she refused them all, saying, "I want someone who loves the Lord more than I do." That sums up the commitment to Christ which is typical among the revival people. One young man was not satisfied with tithing one tenth of his income to the Lord and God's work; he insisted on giving one fifth, saying, "It's the least I can give to a God who gave everything for me." No wonder such people are leading the way in this moral revival.

An evangelist was asked to give an address to members of a swell London club. He began by saying, "Gentlemen, the entrance fee to the kingdom of heaven is nothing. The annual subscription is — everything." It costs nothing to become a Christian — salvation is free — but it costs all we've got to be a Christian in the real sense of the word.

Jesus doesn't want a corner of our lives; he wants full control. The Word of God is capturing many today in this revival. Whenever Christ comes in through his Word and rules a person, that person becomes living evidence of the presence and power of the almighty love of God at work in this world. God wants us to surrender to him, totally and continuously.

When Leonardo da Vinci was painting the great fresco of the Last Supper on the wall of a monastery in Milan, he decorated one corner of the large painting with a little ship. Many people came to see him at work and they admired the little ship. Leonardo thought about this, and one day he painted the ship out, for he wanted nothing to detract from the central figure in the painting. Jesus must be the central figure in our lives.

Donald Coggan, the former Archbishop of Canterbury, challenged Christians by asking whether, if we were in court charged with being Christian, there would be enough evidence to convict us. In his letter to Timothy Paul clearly outlines his evidence: "You . . . know all about my teaching, my way of life, my purpose, faith, patience, love, endurance, persecutions, sufferings" (2 Timothy 3:10–11). History makes it clear why and how the early church grew. They were totally sold out for God!

The best advertisement for the Kingdom is burning, totally dedicated, committed lives changed by God's grace. Jesus demanded, "He that renounceth not all that he hath, *cannot* be my disciple." One ought to be careful and balanced about such things, but the greatest revival sees the greatest sacrifices.

Juan Carlos Ortiz in one of his books tells of the willingness of church members in Argentina to make their homes, cars, bank accounts and indeed all their possessions available for Jesus. With such love and commitment, it is not surprising to find the Argentinian church a growing one, with one million members.

17

REVIVAL THROUGH PRAYER

I am asked constantly on my travels, "What sort of praying is involved to bring such blessing down as this?" Prayer is extraordinary when Christians do not want or need to go to their beds; when they don't care who gets the praise, so long as God gets the glory; when they seek God first and only then look to others.

We must realize that it is God's pleasure to work through fragile people like ourselves. We need to be confident and specific in our prayers.

Before we do anything else we should pray. I have always remembered this comment on the Acts of the Apostles: "Like us, the early church believed in prayer – but unlike us, they prayed!"

Why not keep a personal notebook of all the answers to prayer in your own life and in that of your fellowship? Then when you are in a moment of need, you can look back on the Lord's guidance and provision in the past.

We are to be like children who ask their parents

again and again for what they cannot have . . . but they still ask!

A minister friend of mine had an old car that was not far off the scrapyard. Knowing he had little money, I said, half-joking, "You had better pray for a new one." "Oh, I am," he said. "I'm praying for a yellow Ford Escort." Now that was specific! And a few weeks later he was given a yellow Ford Escort. Now, of course, God doesn't always answer prayers like that, but then most of us never give him a chance to do so! The Bible is full of examples of men and women who dared to trust God and pray specifically.

LOOK UPWARDS, NOT DOWNWARDS

By admitting our powerlessness and leaning on the living God, we have much victory. There is nothing the devil likes more than to make us so preoccupied with our problems that we take our eyes off the Lord. Sadly, many churches are so concerned about dry rot, lack of income, declining numbers, bad relationships and so on, that they take their eyes off the Lord of the church, whose grace is sufficient, whose strength is displayed to the full in weakness and who is more than able to give us victory. Many Christians get worn out because they try to fight God's battles for him. There is a time to fight, but also a time to "stand firm and see the deliverance the Lord will give you" (2 Chronicles 20:17). There is a place in our praying, we have discovered, when we stop all feverish activity and just stand still and wait for God to act.

An expert who had studied gorillas in Africa passed on this key advice: if a large male gorilla suddenly comes at you out of the undergrowth, then you must simply stand still and look at it! The gorilla is not a vicious animal, and having established the fact that you are trespassing on its territory, it will saunter off. The expert told me that the first time this happened to him, it was the hardest thing in the world just to stand there and look at the gorilla. Every fibre of his being wanted to run! For many of us, faced with a difficult situation, the hardest thing in the world is to do nothing! Every fibre of our activist, evangelical being wants to do something. But from time to time, God says, "Do nothing." And then all the glory goes to him at the end of the day, when people see what God has done in our lives.

When you pray, expect something fresh and totally appropriate for the needs of the moment. I know from my experience of the present revival that God loves to surprise us!

God works as we pray. I recently visited Germany, and it was wonderful to rejoice with the many faithful Christians there who have sacrificed in earnest prayer for the countries of Eastern Europe to be set free. Now, after the fall of the Berlin Wall and the Iron Curtain, there is so much evangelism, joy, freedom and church growth, all because *a few prayed*. Recently a group of revived believers went along the so-called "Peace Wall" in Belfast, praying for a similar miracle.

Christ is the unseen guest at our prayer meetings. *He always hears and answers*. 1 Chronicles 5:20 says, "He answered their prayers, because they trusted in Him."

Do you want to see the power of God released into our nation? *Then you must pray*. Do you want to see God glorifying himself in and through his church? Then you must pray.

Casual, occasional, half-hearted, lukewarm, fits-and-starts praying will not do. Instead, burdened, persistent, sacrificial, prolonged, regular prayer is needed. God has said, "if my people . . . will humble themselves and pray and seek my face . . . then will I hear" (2 Chronicles 7:14). He has promised so much! Enter into the richness of his inheritance.

Come, let us seek the Lord. Come, let us pray. Come, let us call on his name and wait in his presence. In revival praying God's glory and power become pre-eminent. "Not to us, O Lord, not to us but to your name be the glory, because of your love and faithfulness" (Psalm 115:1).

Prayer for revival is no sudden flight of fancy, no spiritual hobby. We are not seeking fame, miracles, success, ease, full churches or financial deliverance. Our greatest desire is "that his glory may dwell in our land" (Psalm 85:9).

PRAYER IS THE KEY

"Prayer is the key to setting the nation free" – that's one of the mottoes of the present revival. Prayer is essential if we are to see God working powerfully today.

Gladys Aylward, the famous missionary, gave this advice: "Whatever you do in life, say your prayers. Don't just talk to God. Be very still and quiet and give him a chance to talk to you – you will be surprised what he has to say."

I once saw a short, sharp sentence written up outside a church, and it had more impact than a whole sermon on the value of prayer for those in trouble. It simply read: "If your knees tremble, kneel on them." The Bible says, "pray in the Spirit on all occasions with all kinds of prayers and requests" (Ephesians 6:18).

Prayer is a gift from God – given to be used. It is a power in the universe as distinct, as real, as natural and as uniform as gravity or light or electricity. We may use it as trustingly as we would use any of these. It is a weapon to be used in strenuous and determined spiritual warfare.

Prayer is universal. We need to keep on praying

for all the saints. In this sense our prayers are to be "catholic" or all-embracing. No professing Christian can legitimately be excluded from our prayers. And we ought to embrace all countries as well as all denominations, making our prayer time an international journey.

Prayer is evangelistic. Paul asked the Ephesian Christians to "Pray also for me, that whenever I open my mouth, words may be given me so that I will fearlessly make known the mystery of the Gospel" (Ephesians 6:19). Similarly today, one of the great burdens of prayer is the spread of the evangel throughout the world: in the secularized West, in post-Marxist Eastern Europe, in the Islamic nations, in China, and elsewhere in the world. Through prayer we can conduct an evangelistic campaign in any and every country of the world! We can become actively involved in the evangelization of nations which prohibit missionaries and ban churches. Remember — all significant movements for God have had their origin in prayer.

A man sent a letter he had typed; the machine had one faulty key, so the letter read:

Xvxn though my typxwritxr is an old modxl, it works wxll xnough xxcxpt for onx of thx kxys. I havx wishxd many timxs that it workxd pxrfxctly. It is trux thxrx arx forty-fivx kxys that function wxll xnough, but just onx kxy not working makxs all thx diffxrxncx. So, nxxt timx you think you arx only onx pxrson and that your xffort is not nxxdxd, rxmxmbxr my typxwritxr, and say to yoursxlf, "I am a kxy pxrson, thx Lord nxxds mx."

Yes, indeed, we do all count. The Lord needs you. In prayer *you count*, you are vital. You are the "key" to the Kingdom, using God's ultimate weapon — prayer.

18

KEYS TO REVIVAL

In this chapter I want us to think about some of the prerequisites for revival: faith, humility, persistence and paying the price.

FAITH

God always responds to true faith. He will do anything for a few people of faith who really believe. Faith believes that God is a speaking God, that he wants to guide, direct, prosper and free us. Faith stands on its feet and claims victory; it claims on the strength of what God has said and done. Faith knows that the Father can do all things. Faith is a philosophy of life which is diametrically opposed to secular thinking. "Faith is being sure of what we hope for and certain of what we do not see" (Hebrews 11:1). Faith never gives up; it presses on and on and on until it wins.

I like the story of the English tourist and the old Highland shepherd. The tourist was recuperating after a nervous breakdown and was trying desperately to find not only health and strength, but also courage to battle on and faith in God. It was then that he met with the old shepherd. They walked and talked together, and the tourist, looking up the mountains from the track in the valley, remarked, "I suppose there's no way over those heights?" "Oh, but there is," replied the shepherd. "You can't see it from the valley, but if you follow the winding track and keep plodding on and up you'll cross the ridge and reach the further side." It was just the message the tourist needed. He plodded on and got over the hills. He also persisted in reading the Bible and through it found faith in God. Thus he got over the hill of illness, despair and failure and began to live a refreshing, healthy, happy, victorious Christian life.

A famous writer told the following story:

It was many years ago and I had a decision to make which could affect my whole life. Now, when I have a problem I like to get away to a quiet place, and think. In this case, I went to our local park. I sat down on a bench, and looked up at the tall trees, their branches towering above me. That was when I saw the squirrel – jumping from one high branch to another. At one point, he appeared to be aiming for a limb so far out of reach that his leap looked like suicide. He missed

– I gasped – but he landed, safely and unconcerned, on a branch several feet lower. Then he climbed upward to his goal and all was well. An elderly man sitting at the other end of the bench said, "Funny, I've seen dozens of them jump like that. A lot of them miss, but I've never seen one coming to any harm." Then he chuckled, "I suppose they've just got to risk if if they don't want to spend their lives on the same branch." That's it, I thought – a squirrel has to take a chance when scaling the heights every day. . . Should I not do the same? My decision was made; and time was to prove that it was the right one.

Faith is to risk all, not to stay and play safe on the same old branch, but to take the leap of faith.

We don't want miracles merely for their own sake, but to show that God is a God of miracles. For instance, Elijah the prophet's real desire was to see signs and wonders "so these people will know that you, O Lord, are God, and that you are turning their hearts back again" (1 Kings 18:37). This is reckless faith from a man abandoned to a God who never leaves us in the lurch when we seek his honour in the midst of mass compromise. Only a big experience of the Holy Spirit and a wholehearted commitment to apply the Scriptures to our lives can make this possible, but it is possible to believing hearts.

Thank God for the rebirth of faith in countless hearts across the land!

HUMILITY

The church in this land has reached rock bottom in many places. God has allowed his people to come to an end of themselves, to be humbled in the very depths.

J. B. Phillips translates 1 Peter 5:5, "Clothe yourselves with humility", as "Wear the overall of humility in serving each other". This reminds us that humbleness is not just some starry-eyed quality, but is the practical, down-to-earth business of doing what we can to help one another. Henry Ward Beecher once said, "Religion means work; it means hard work; it means work in a dirty world. The world has to be cleaned by somebody and you are not really called of God unless you are prepared to scour and scrub." Put on your overalls!

Humble people will do anything for God. This revival is humbling many of God's people into the very dust at times.

Charles Haddon Spurgeon was a very famous Baptist preacher and is generally agreed to have been one of the greatest orators of the nineteenth century. Though he was accustomed to being the principal speaker before great audiences, Spurgeon never lost his admiration for those not so much in the public eye. One day he wrote this little verse: "It needs more skill than I can tell, To play the second fiddle well." Our job may be quite a lowly one. We may not get any public recognition, but let us do it to the very best of our ability.

Here is an old Scottish saying which makes us all take a new look at ourselves: "When God measures a man he puts the tape around the heart, not the head."

God is humbling his people – it is a key factor in the revival today. The words of Zephaniah the prophet are being fulfilled in the 1990s: "I will take away from your midst those who rejoice . . . and you shall no longer be haughty. . . I will leave in your midst a meek and humble people, and they shall trust in the name of the Lord. . . The remnant . . . shall do no unrighteousness . . . speak no lies, nor shall a deceitful tongue be found in their mouth, and no one shall make them afraid." Today the people of God are being brought low so that they may know him and demonstrate his power to this generation. "Humble yourselves, therefore, under God's mighty hand, that he may lift you up in due time" (1 Peter 5:6).

PERSISTENCE

A Derbyshire town recently became the focus of a remarkable mission that awoke the sleepy area.

Crowds of people flocked to church, and many were cured of their sicknesses. The local newspapers gave the mission plenty of coverage, with many accounts of hitherto sick and disabled people walking away from services after being cured by prayer.

The story behind the church is a fascinating one and shows the importance of being persistent. The pastor had faithfully run the little mission for twenty years, but little impact could be made on the indifferent town. He had a congregation of six people! He tried everything, he worked hard, he preached well, but finally he gave in, as there was no growth.

Then, just prior to his retirement, the local council badly needed to extend the road outside his church building. He refused adamantly to let them have it at any price, unless they gave him a new building with full facilities such as a car park, a youth hall, offices and so forth on a prime site. After lengthy legal debates, they gave in. He was able to open the brand new building, still with only six people, and handed it over to his young successor, feeling that something worthwhile had been achieved.

For a year the new pastor struggled as his predecessor had, but he could not crack the hardness of materialistic hearts. Then he invited my team and me to lead a week-long mission. A hundred people came on the first night. Over thirty were converted, which was a very good start, but then when a lady left her wheelchair and walked, *the mission took off!* Two nights later we were crammed, and over two hundred people were converted. It became the talk of the town; there was a new interest in the miracle church. *The pastor's persistence had paid off.*

After I left, the young pastor walked the streets, visited those who had been touched by God, invited people to his home for coffee, started meetings every day of the week, talked with unsaved husbands, built up confidence in the Word in weak believers, brought biblical assurance to the floundering, and opened up the church day and night for meals, young wives' Bible classes and tea times.

When I revisited the church less than a year later, a hundred and thirty people were regularly attending, meetings were held every day of the week, and the church doors were hardly ever closed. It had become a burning, blazing, Holy Ghost revival centre! Now speakers come from the USA, South Africa and elsewhere to minister in this renowned centre. None of this would have happened without the persistence of the old pastor and his young successor.

A farmer was once teaching his nephew how to cultivate corn. The two of them set out across the field in a tractor, the boy at the wheel. He was doing very well until they hit a marshy spot and the wheels began to slip in the mud. Immediately the boy slowed down and looked at his uncle for instructions. But the uncle yelled, "Don't slow down now – give it gas and go on through!"

That is sound advice for you and me in our quest for success. The marshy spots on the path to God's destination are the places where we most need to persevere, to "give it gas and go on through". If we stop we will start to sink. And there is no reason to stop. We won't run out of gas – in fact, God has seen to it that our "tractor" is able to take us safely over the roughest terrain. Let me remind you of that powerful passage from the letter to the Romans:

> Who shall separate us from the love of Christ? Shall trouble or hardship or persecution or famine or nakedness or danger or sword? As it is written: "For your sake we face death all day long; we are considered as sheep to be slaughtered." No, in all these things we are more than conquerors through him who loved us.
>
> (Romans 8:35–37)

God wants you to be a conqueror. Think about that. He's not going to do all the fighting for you – you have to do that yourself, for the conquest must be yours.

The missionaries Carey, Judson and Morrison each toiled for years in their respective mission fields before they saw their first convert.

The father of the animated cartoon, Walt Disney,

became great because as a child he was rewarded by an old man for drawing a picture of a horse. The dollar and the encouragement he received inspired him to earn a living as a cartoonist. But although he got a job with a newspaper, he was fired shortly afterwards. "You haven't got any talent," the boss told him. "Why don't you get out of the drawing business?" But Walt remembered the encouragement given to him by the old man, and so carried on drawing. He refused to quit.

When he started as a writer Scott Fitzgerald received so many rejection slips from publishers that he papered his room with them! One day, when yet another publisher's letter arrived, he was just about to throw it on the fire when a friend took it out of his hand and opened it. It was a good job he did – finally a publisher had agreed to print one of Fitzgerald's books! It became a bestseller.

Thomas Mart originally thought it would take him three years to discover the secret of refrigeration. In the end it took him twenty-seven. During that time he kept a motto on the cornice in his living room: "To persevere is to succeed." He did succeed. Before he died he saw the first refrigerated ship leave to pick up meat from Australia.

The New Testament contains numerous passages encouraging us to endure difficulty. It's not whether you start the race that counts, but whether you finish. As Paul wrote to the Galatians: "Let us not become weary in doing good, for at the proper time we will reap a harvest if we do not give up. Therefore, as we have opportunity, let us do good to all people. . ." (Galatians 6:9–10).

So "give it gas and go on through". It's very easy to become disspirited, to think that the marshes cover the entire field. But don't be fooled. They don't. Down times, hard experiences and bitter lessons are bound to come to us, but they don't last forever. The important thing is to keep going. As the Psalmist points out, tears may last for a night, but joy comes with the morning. To be a conqueror is to keep those tears in perspective. It is to know that as you move on, difficulties will give way to resounding success. Indeed, they can do nothing else, for you have Christ himself within you, strengthening you to do "all things".

God wants you to be conqueror. He wants you to be a success. He wants you to have peace and faith in him. He wants you to come out on top. That is the sort of Christian life that honours him. He has said: "To him who conquers I will grant to eat of the tree of life. . . He who conquers, I will make him a pillar in the temple of my God" (Revelation 2:7, 3:12). This is the spirit that is being repeated many times across our nation, by people like the young Derbyshire pastor, and it is bringing revival in the hardest of places.

PAYING THE PRICE

It was a simple, happy, charming service. The organist played the Wedding March, and the bridegroom kissed the bride. Then they all went into the vestry. Suddenly and impulsively the bride turned to her father and gave him two kisses – one on the cheek, and one on his right hand. That hand was deformed and unpleasant to look at; a rather shapeless hand, with unnaturally pink flesh. "Oh Daddy," she whispered, tears in her happy eyes, "but for your dear, dear hand, I'd never have known such happiness today." With that hand, over twenty years before, her father had rescued his baby daughter from a fire. It had cost him dearly to save her.

In the present revival many Christians are making sacrifices and paying a high price in order to see the mighty working of God's Spirit. Meanwhile other Christians are finding it hard to accept that revival is costly. It goes against the grain to have to face obstacles and adversity. Trials show what is in us!

We can lose our first love while we retain our good works; we can lose our fresh, living faith and still keep up a jolly good show. Gradually the joy, excitement, passion and vision fade away, but we are still plodding along and faithful. Almost imperceptibly, we have stopped changing and growing. But Paul says, "where the Spirit of the Lord is, there is freedom. And we, who with unveiled faces all reflect the Lord's glory, are being transformed into his likeness with ever-increasing glory, which comes from the Lord, who is the Spirit" (2 Corinthians 3:17–18). What an exciting prospect for any child of God! To be conformed into Christ's image simply means willingness to suffer, to win through.

According to a very old story, there was once a Roman youth who was given a sword by his father. After some practice with it, he complained that the sword was too short. "In that case," said his father, "you must add a step to it." I like that. It may be that in the battle of life you lack skill or money or influence, and you imagine that because your sword is too short you cannot win a victory. But if you add a step to it – if you go forward bravely, get nearer to the problem, fight harder, or wait more patiently, give your heart and mind and strength to the immediate task – the chances are that, ill-equipped though you may be, you will win through. It is not so much the length of the sword that counts – it is the determination of the fighter.

In the revival we face many obstacles, discouragements and trials. As Paul wrote, "We are hard pressed on every side, but not crushed; . . . struck down, but not destroyed" (2 Corinthians 4:8–9).

A bishop's remark at a Confirmation Service was "Participation in the Holy Communion is not a luxury for the devout. It is preparation for sacrifice and for battle."

"Sacrifice" is not a popular word. Even when people see this present revival — the growth of churches, many conversions, outstanding testimonies, miraculous healing power, magnificent worship — they do not grasp that it is all through sacrifice.

In January 1970, Gladys Aylward died at the age of sixty-eight on the island of Taiwan. A few weeks earlier one of the orphans she had brought up on the Chinese mainland visited her and asked what she wanted for a Christmas gift. She said she would like a cotton quilt. But when the temperature dropped to forty degrees below freezing point, she gave her new quilt to an orphan and her mattress to her Chinese housemaid. When she died, all that she had was one worn-out blanket. She had given everything else away.

Jesus said, "whoever wants to save his life will lose it, but whoever loses his life for me and for the gospel will save it" (Mark 8:35).

One day during the First World War a doctor was chatting with a young soldier who had just arrived from France. The soldier was carrying a load which seemed too much even for a big, healthy lad, and the doctor wondered how he could trudge along in such heavy boots with so much on his shoulders. "How far can you march with all that?" asked the doctor. The boy promptly replied, "Oh, about twelve miles, sir." Then, as an afterthought, he added, "But fifteen with a band!" Similarly, Christians weighed down with work and worry on a hard road can go farther and endure more if a bit of faith enables them to keep a song in their heart.

A man once made a huge kite, but when he tried to fly it, it kept swooping down to earth. An old fisherman who was watching told him to tie a weight to its tail, and when this had been done the kite flew beautifully. The man was surprised: he had expected that the weight would hold the kite down, not help it to rise. Often it is the things that we count as heavy and burdensome which in fact can lift us up in faith and hope.

Let us climb every moutain, scale each hill of trouble and adversity, until, reaching the heights with God, we live above all hindrances, trials and oppositions. This is being experienced by many in this great revival – *but the price is high*.

19

THREE PIECES OF ADVICE

In this chapter I would like to offer some advice on three crucial areas of concern in the present revival. Those areas are: how to deal with God's silences; the importance of not wasting time; and the control of the tongue.

GOD'S SILENCES

A little girl went to church with her mother; they often popped into the ancient building for a quiet prayer, when out shopping. It was always empty, and the little girl commented, "Why is God always out when we call?" Sometimes in the Christian life it can seem as if "God is out"; he seems not to hear us, he seems to be silent. For decades British Christians cried out to God for revival – through the turbulent 1950s, the permissive 1960s, the disturbed 1970s, and the violent 1980s. Now, in the 1990s, revival is here at last! But why did we have to wait so long? Why did God seem to be silent? Christians of the past sought for what we see now, and planned, and waited, but it did not come. They were more faithful and holy people than we are, yet the heavens seemed silent.

We all go through hardships and difficult times when God seems a long way off. We can say with Richard III in Shakespeare's play, "I am like one in a thorny wood." The message is clear: though God is invisible, he is invincible and always working out what is best for his people. When David Watson lay dying, the Bishop of Southwark sent a message to him: "One of the mysteries of the Christian faith is His silence."

Often God's people have found themselves enveloped in a fog that has muffled God's voice. To suffer the silence of God in the presence of injustice can be truly disorientating. God is just, yes, but just in his own time, and in between there are gaps of silence.

Sometimes the silence of God is deafening. It was deafening for 400 years between the books of Genesis and Exodus. The time of Samuel's birth, when the word of the Lord was rare and visions were infrequent, was a difficult time. The 400-year-long silence between Malachi and Matthew was also deafening. The silence of Heaven when Jesus hung on the Cross was the most momentous of all silences in history.

Maybe you are experiencing a similar enigma.

How could God be so silent when you cry out to him so loudly, so desperately? Why doesn't he answer? Why doesn't he call out from the shore so that you can orient yourself in the fog that has enveloped you? He wants us to learn that the periods of his silence are just as significant as the times when he speaks. God is not as distant as you think! We are never out of his watchful eye.

A sailor was once shipwrecked. He prayed and struggled to survive alone. He painstakingly constructed a hut with a few things he salvaged from the wreck and from whatever he could find on the island. That little hut was the only protection he had from the harsh elements. Upon returning one evening from a lengthy search for food, he was terrified to find the hut engulfed in flames. The loss devastated him. He spent that night despondent, sleeping on the sand. He awoke early the next morning and, to his surprise, saw a ship anchored off the island. A crew member stepped ashore and told him, "We saw your smoke signal and came to rescue you." What had seemed to be a destruction turned out to be a deliverance.

The disciples thought that the day of Jesus' crucifixion was the darkest day of their lives, but his death was followed by his resurrection! God is not distant or indifferent. He sees, he cares. He intervenes on our behalf. He can use the strangest situations and circumstances to the advantage of his people. Learn that when all seems lost, it isn't. When no one seems to notice, God does. When God seems absent, he is there – in sickness or health, in poverty or prosperity, in the darkest night or the brightest day.

Don't be disturbed by the silent times. *Wait patiently for God to act*. "No eye has seen, no ear has heard, no mind has conceived what God has prepared for those who love him" (1 Corinthians 2:9). God has come again in our day to *his waiting people*.

GOD NOTICES, WE
(HAVE TO PATIENTLY WAIT)

DON'T WASTE TIME

Most of us will not play a crucial role in history, but we are called to serve Christ faithfully day by day, regardless of what we do. John Wesley was asked by a friend, "John, suppose you knew you were going to die by midnight tomorrow. How would you spend your time until then?" "I would spend it,"Wesley replied, "exactly as I expect to spend it now. I would preach tonight in Gloucester, get up early tomorrow morning and proceed to Tewkesbury, where I would preach in the afternoon. Then I would go to the Martins' house in the evening, talk with Mr Martin, pray with the family, retire, putting myself in the Father's care, and wake up in heaven." He was ready, he would change nothing, his time was used as God wanted.

To live such a God-centred life, self-surrendered, means that whatever way we go in making decisions, or however we use our time, it will all come out right in the end. A revived heart walking in faith is never surprised at God's timing. Revival usually comes unexpectedly. Charles Lamb wrote: "Not so many sounds exceed in interest a knock at the door." God's knock at the door has come.

Time is a priceless gift from God. We should guard it with care and use it to the fullest. David Brainerd, the faithful missionary to the American Indians, said, "Oh how precious is time; and how guilty it makes me feel when I think I have trifled away and misimproved it, or neglected to fill up each part of it with duty, to the utmost of my ability and capacity."

In his book, *Lest Ye Faint*, Franklin Logsdon tells of the president of a Christian college who entered the chapel service one morning with a solemn expression on his face. Following the hymn, he stood up to speak to the student body. He said, "I have just received a telephone message bearing sad news. A fine young man who graduated from this school three years ago has died suddenly." A hush fell over the audience. The president asked the students, "If all you desire to do, if all you hope to do, had to be crowded into three short years, what would you do differently today?"

He who has no vision of eternity doesn't know

the value of time. Soon the harvest time will be past;
what will you pack into your short life? God's time
of the latter rain will soon be over, and Judgement
will be here. Time is very short, God is saving now,
the redeeming time is here.

Ministers used to say to me, when they were
seeking advice on coming into the ministry for the
first time, "How do you spend your time?" I never
seem to be asked that today. People in God's work
– workers, believers and ministers – are often finding a new appreciation of time. The sense of short-
ness of time, the exciting, fresh, reviving spirit
amongst so many of God's people, is revealing and
producing new disciplines.

This is God's Day! Appreciate this time of revival;
don't waste it in idle pleasure, selfish interests,
worthless gossip or wasteful self-indulgence. Time
is short – revival is here! Let us be, as the prophet
said, "Willing in the day of his power". Spurgeon
wrote, "We dilly-dally around . . . why do we waste
od's time, when we ought to be doing?"

I like the last prayer of the outstanding Scots
preacher Peter Marshall, Chaplain to the US Senate:
"Deliver us, our Father, from futile hopes, and from
clinging to lost causes, that we may move into ever
growing calm and ever widening horizons . . . for
small deeds done are better than great deeds planned. We know we cannot do everything, but help
us to do something for Jesus' sake. Amen."

Time would teach us one great lesson, and that is the value of waiting patiently for God. Revival seems to have been a millennium coming. Patiently we worked, preached and prayed for decades, and now, at last, revival has come. But why now? Why such a long wait? Habakkuk reminds us, "the revelation awaits an appointed time. . . Though it linger, wait for it; it will certainly come" (Habakkuk 2:3).

The famous French writer Jean de la Bruyere, who knew something about the struggle of life, wrote,"There is no road too long to the man who advances deliberately and without undue haste." The Psalmist noted, "I waited patiently for the Lord; and he inclined unto me, and heard my cry."

The waiting for revival is now over. Don't waste your time in this, God's Day. Instead commit yourself to working with God in this present mighty move of his Spirit.

CONTROL YOUR TONGUE

The church has long been bedevilled by the tongue. It has "caused most of man's trouble", said Martin Luther. Division, unloving words, discouragement, pessimism, defeatism, strife – all these come from uncontrolled tongues.

It is just three inches long, but it can bring down a big, strong man! Be careful with the tongue. It has the power to bless or hurt, to comfort or curse, to heal or wound.

God doesn't necessarily want silence, but control. James wrote, "The tongue . . . is a fire, a world of evil among the parts of the body. It corrupts the whole person, sets the whole course of his life on fire . . ." (James 3:6). How powerful indeed is the tongue. If tempted to speak unkindly, the best rule is to leave those words on the tip of your tongue.

The tongue can be used for flattery, gossip, pride, boasting, criticism, slander, anger, temper and exaggeration; or you can use it to speak of love, inspiration, blessing, joy, praise, encouragement and wisdom.

I've seen the tongue wreck a minister's ministry, bringing "big" preachers into the gutter. I've seen it wreck a courtship and bring heartbreak – through a few stupid words. I've seen it divide a family who were once so close – through a hasty word. I've seen it split hundreds of churches – through hurtful, bombastic, dogmatic, loveless words. I've heard and read of words wrecking whole nations and causing world wars, killing millions of innocent people.

I was challenged on a live national radio programme in New Zealand to show in words and power that God does work miracles today, by praying there and then for some sick people. I accepted the challenge, although nervously, weakly, humbly.

God used words of power over the airwaves of New Zealand. As I prayed, God took up my poor words, and the sick, the blind, the crippled, the arthritic and the pain-riddled were *instantly healed* on the show! This caused a sensation, and soon miracles spread across the nation. Thousands flocked to our revival meetings. Words of power, anointed by the Holy Ghost, make all the difference.

James Galway with his tongue and flute can charm the world. A Saddam Hussein can curse the world with division, hate, violence, lust and heart-ache! Your words can be salt-water or fresh, living, refreshing water. They can be poisonous as wild berries, or as lush as rich, sweet fruit.

Lady Astor once said accusingly to Winston Churchill, "You are drunk!" Churchill replied, "You are ugly, madam, and I shall be sober in the morning." We must be careful with our words.

In my ministry, whether I am travelling, or eating in a restaurant, or enjoying hospitality in someone's home, or talking with the press, or preaching, or praying for sick people, I know that I must constantly watch my tongue; I must be careful about what I say and what I commit myself to.

Christians are what they eat; they are what they have been fed by their ministers. Pastor, what are your folk like? Do they have big hearts, a big vision; are they loving, full of fire? Or are they critical, dried-up, hair-splitting, loveless, undisciplined?

Remember, we ministers are responsible to God for what we teach our folk.

Where the fire of the revival is most intense, God is dominating his people's hearts, minds and *tongues!*

Two great boxers slogged it out for the heavy-weight championship of the world, the prize £10 million. After a bruising, painful battle, one hand was raised, and he walked home conqueror. When he got to his house, he gave his wife the £10 million, and she was *MORE THAN CONQUEROR!* It's time to win with a full revival. A time to weep, a time to tremble at His Presence, a time for joy, A TIME TO BE MORE THAN CONQUERORS! We have the full adequacy of the Blood and Atonement of our Lord Jesus Christ. He died so that no one may be shackled or bound. Jesus never leaves anyone the same as he finds them. The ANOINTING OF THE HOLY SPIRIT destroys the enemy. Revival is CHRIST REIGNING VICTORIOUS, it is a flood of divine biblical light. It puts down Satan. THE GREAT GLORY IS GOD'S. If you are not in revival – search, cry, weep, be broken, pray – for GOD HAS SAID –

"I *HAVE HEARD THEIR CRY FOR* I *KNOW THEIR SORROWS".* (Exodus 3:7)

THE DAWN HAS COME!

10 MILLION FOR JESUS IN THE UK BY YEAR 2000

Here is one of the most daring visions ever attempted in this nation: to reach and seek to turn one-fifth of Britain's population to Christ by the end of this century.

IT CAN BE DONE
Melvin is aiming at this. Help him, invite him to your town, pray for his team daily. Write to him today:

The Rev. Melvin Banks, Crusade Office, 44 Monks Way, Cricketts Meadow, Chippenham, Wiltshire SN15 3TT, England

———

Don't miss Melvin's life story – *Nothing Is Impossible to God* – planned for 1994: "The Acts of the Apostles today in the UK."